THE 100 BEST
INTERIORS IN COLOUR

BETA-PLUS

THE 100 BEST
INTERIORS IN COLOUR

CONTENTS

A timeless appearance 6
In French style 8
The effective use of lime paints. 10
The metamorphosis of the Chateau de Vierset 12
An intimate atmosphere 14
An ode to country living 16
Handmade craftsmanship as a guiding principle. 18
A passion for the Burgundy-region 26
Harmony of colour and texture. 28
Traditional fine artists 30
La vie en rose 32
Dramatic green. 34
Poetic kitchens 36
As though risen from the ashes 38
Complete restoration of a 19th-century long-fronted farmhouse 40
Transformation of a 200-year-old farmhouse into a classic contemporary country home .42
Rehabilitation. 44
Chateau Castigno 46
A sanctuary of peace. 60
A colourful country retreat 62
A timeless English manor 64
Paris *pied-à-terre* 66
Inspired by Amsterdam 70
A different guesthouse 74
A perfect symbiosis. 76
A triplex apartment in Paris 78
A country house near Brussels 80
A real symbiosis 82
Dark is beautiful. 84
Chez Odette 86
Renovation of a historic finca 88
The contemporary renovation of a former hunting lodge 90
A blend of timeless and contemporary: a balanced philosophy for living. 92
The revival of a 19th-century castle 94
A stately country villa near Antwerp. 96
A very tasteful B&B 98
Anglo-Saxon inspiration. 100
A cosy and sober apartment in a 17th-century listed building. 102
A subtle colour palette 104
Renovation of a typical Flemish country house 106

A new life	108
A joyful family home	110
An apartment in Geneva	112
Cosmopolitan feeling	116
A house in the Luxembourg countryside	118
A country house in the Kempen Woodland	120
Newly built and still authentic	124
Timeless minimalism in a traditional farmhouse	126
An interior with a soul	128
A love of art, antiques and traditional crafts	132
An exceptional country house for passionate antiquarians	134
A distinctive new villa in wooded surroundings	136
A sophisticated sense of colour	138
Living amongst colours: the authenticity of lime paints	140
Streamlined, classic and chic	142
A recently built country house with an age-old patina	148
A tasteful renovation of a historic notary's house	150
Living and working in perfect harmony	152
Soul and feeling	154
A unique blend	156
Cosy living	158
The beauty of lime paints	160
A classic villa with contemporary details	164
Family life	166
A discrete metamorphosis	168
A successful start	170
The metamorphosis of a farmhouse into a country manor house	172
A perfect balance between classic and modern	174
A fascinating mix of old and new	176
Space and light in a contemporary country house	182
The attractions of an ancient farmhouse	184
A unique country house in Flemish style	186
Restoration of an 18th century brewery	192
A passion for beauty	196
Light, spacious and sunny	200
A symbiosis of old and new	202
Restructuring an apartment in a Haussmannian building	206
Haute couture in a home in the heart of Paris	208
Soft colours in a restored farmhouse	212
Source of inspiration	222

A TIMELESS APPEARANCE

Antiques Amber was founded almost forty years ago by Paul Wagemans. He started searching for antique furniture and architectural antiques. His projects grew in size and the same clients were also asking for new timberwork with an old patina. Today the family company has grown to a well-known house for architectural antiques and interior architecture. Antiques Amber concentrates on craftsmanship and traditional made-to-measure work: a focus on quality that is getting very rare in this industrial age. Quality can be found in many old objects and materials: they offer a timeless appearance which is mainly accomplished by the love for the craft.

www.antiekamber.be

IN FRENCH STYLE

Over recent years, Costermans has built up a solid reputation as
a construction company for exclusive villa projects.
The house in this report, built in a French style, is a good example of Costermans'
working methods: the use of durable materials throughout, together with enthusiasm,
skill and a strong focus on the interior, with a timelessly classic design.

www.costermans-projecten.be

In the bathroom old Bianco Perlino marble on the floor has been combined with the Dark Emperador marble of the surfaces.

↖
The entrance hall with its old floor design combining French white stone and slate. Elegant staircase with wrought-iron balusters.

THE EFFECTIVE USE OF LIME PAINTS

Arte Constructo, based in Schelle, has made a name for itself on the restoration market as an international distributor of mineral, natural and biological products such as Unilit (natural hydraulic lime), Coridecor (fine finishing products based on lime putty) and Keim (silicate paints).

www.arteconstructo.be

THE METAMORPHOSIS OF THE CHÂTEAU DE VIERSET

The Château de Vierset has an eventful history. The building, a fortified castle and farm with four towers, was mentioned for the first time in 1090, under the name of "Versaih". It was torched by Prince Bishop Henri van Gelder and later, in around 1775, rebuilt by General de Billehé, knight of the Order of Malta and owner of the famous Vierset regiment, which was in Austrian service. In 1818, the castle passed into the hands of François-Charles de Mercy-Argenteau, Napoleon's chamberlain. It remained in the family until 1877. A number of different families subsequently owned the property: d'Overschie de Neerysche, Lamarche and Lamalle.

www.chateaudevierset.be

A number of sitting rooms in authentic materials. These rooms are set aside for seminars and other events.

The hallway and the upstairs sitting room with fabric walls and ethnic art. Old Brazilian jugs on a table with an Indian oxcart as a base.

AN INTIMATE ATMOSPHERE

Costermans built this classic country house in the green countryside surrounding Antwerp. Historic building materials were used consistently throughout the project, lending the house a timeless and intimate atmosphere.

www.costermans-projecten.be

An antique table now used as a desk. The floor is in antique planks of solid French oak.

An oak staircase in English style with wrought-iron balusters fastened to the wall with rose-shaped ornaments.

This door in glass and wrought iron leads to the wine cellar and tasting area.
On the floor are antique terracotta flagstones.

↖
An old oriental door on a simple metal base has been transformed into a coffee table.

AN ODE TO COUNTRY LIVING

This beautiful country house with a meadow view is the result of a very close collaboration between Porte Bonheur and Natalie Haegeman Interiors. Ingrid Segers and Annemie Coppens, the founders of Porte Bonheur, had this house built in a rustic style with an emphasis on the use of old materials. The house was then furnished by NH-Interiors, with an atmosphere of warmth and cosiness as the aim.

www.nataliehaegeman-interiors.be   www.portebonheur.be

Oak floors and an old-oak beamed ceiling, which was subsequently painted, were chosen for the living room. The coffee table is made from an 18th-century door with a wrought-iron base from Venice. Antique kelims from Turkey. The open fireplace has been rendered in lime.

↖
The walls in the TV room also have a lime finish. As throughout the rest of the house, the colours were chosen on the spot.
Coffee table in 19th-century oak; wall light made from old ironwork.
In the centre of the wall on this page, two symmetrical steel windows.

The bathroom and shower are in tadelakt. The concrete washbasin has been given a special finish.

HANDMADE CRAFTSMANSHIP
AS A GUIDING PRINCIPLE

In this report on the stone company Van den Weghe – The Stonecompany a few recent projects are shown with handmade craftsmanship as a guiding principle: perfection in custom-made stone as a result of over thirty years' experience in the top segment.

www.vandenweghe.be

Kitchen work surfaces in bleached Rose Aurore marble with a massive hewn sink. All design and furniture: Joris Van Apers.

A kitchen with a La Cornue stove and a work surface and floor in white Carrara marble.

The Alhambra of the Low Countries!
These wellness rooms in a private country house are clad in Moroccan zeliges and Golden Brown as the main marble. Golden Brown was also chosen for around the jacuzzi (realized by Antheunis).

A PASSION FOR THE BURGUNDY-REGION

Bourgondisch Kruis offers one of the most extensive collections of Burgundy slabs and natural stone, which can be used to make such features as floors, stairs, fireplaces and columns. The Bourgondisch Kruis team adapts these historic construction materials for use in a great variety of restoration projects. The company has its own carpentry workshop for this purpose - where experienced professionals produce perfect custom-made work based around oak panels – and a stonemason's where Burgundy limestone and bluestone are turned into, for example, kitchen work surfaces, exclusive floor and wall cladding and solid washbasins.

www.bourgondisch-kruis.be

This orangery was realised completely according to a design by Bourgondisch Kruis.
The hood construction in solid antique oak and the authentic Burgundy flagstones were also supplied by Bourgondisch Kruis.
The windows are made from wrought iron.

HARMONY OF COLOUR AND TEXTURE

The family business of Eddy and Vera Dankers form a perfect tandem. Eddy Dankers runs Dankers Decor, one of the country's most reputable traditional painting companies and has been a royal supplier for many years. Vera manages Dankers Creation, an interior design agency that produces handmade home textiles and curtains in a completely traditional way. The interior in this report was designed by Vera Dankers and painted by Dankers Decor with lime paints from Arte Constructo.

www.dankers.be

The walls in the toilet were prepared by hand by Dankers Decor and coloured with natura pigments. The blinds in the hall are made from kilim fabric.

The armchair is upholstered in purple silk, the sofa and chairs in white velvet, the blinds in white linen.

TRADITIONAL FINE ARTISTS

The team of Bert De Waal, fine artists in traditional painting techniques, has realized this project in Corical lime paint from Arte Constructo in a house designed by Themenos.

www.dewaalverf.be   www.arteconstructo.be

The fine artists de Waal used a technique in Corical lime paint in a project by Themenos.

LA VIE EN ROSE

The Dutch kitchen company Paul van de Kooi has designed and produced this very special kitchen: all cupboards are finished with pink gloss paints.

www.paulvandekooi.nl

La vie en rose: birch laminate interiors and fronts in solid oak, with a pink gloss finish. The concrete work surface was cast in situ. Stove and fridge-freezer by Viking.

DRAMATIC GREEN

This kitchen is the heart of the home for a family with two children. The classic table and chairs have been replaced by a combination of a bench and table in American walnut wood. The work surface is in Italian Calacatta marble.
All of the appliances are built into the dramatic green wall. The floor is in slate tiles.

www.wilfra.be

35

POETIC KITCHENS

Anne De Visscher and her husband Eric Meert started designing and creating kitchens in 1996, specialising in classic country kitchens with a timeless atmosphere. They gave their company a poetic name: *Il Etait Une Fois* (Once Upon a Time). All of their creations conform to the highest standards of quality: each kitchen is individually designed to reflect the needs and requirements of the client. The units are painted after installation in a finish that harmonises with the colours throughout the rest of the home.

"Le Cottage" with walls painted in antique black and ash-grey (Argile). Fitted furniture with pale grey Argile finish. Work surfaces in a honed finish with a contoured edge. On the floor, old terracotta tomettes. A double washbasin from Villeroy & Boch. Franke taps. The wall behind the Lacanche stove (model: Chambertin in mandarin) is in old tomettes, combined with bluestone cabochons.
Furniture knobs in old nickel.

AS THOUGH RISEN FROM THE ASHES

The Brabant farm in this report appears to have been standing for centuries, but appearances can be deceptive: this country house was completely constructed with old building materials by architect Stéphane Boens. Boens took inspiration for this project from the authentic eighteenth-century farmhouses that were common in Walloon Brabant: a long driveway leading to an entrance gate that would open out on to an inner courtyard with a main building and several outbuildings.

www.stephaneboens.be

The team of Axel Vervoordt, the renowned antiques dealer and interior designer, was responsible for selecting the curtains and chairs, in close consultation with architect Stéphane Boens.

In the breakfast corner, the architect shows a fondness for natural, rustic materials.
The monochrome white colour palette lends a contemporary cachet.
The paintings are by artist Caroline Ancion.

↖
A fascinating contrast between the sophisticated materials and furnishings and the informal, rural surroundings.

COMPLETE RESTORATION
OF A 19TH-CENTURY LONG-FRONTED FARMHOUSE

This nineteenth-century long-fronted farmhouse (ca. 1850), situated in Oisterwijk (near Tilburg) in the south of the Netherlands, has been completely restored to create a distinctive country house. The restoration was particularly thorough: only the exterior walls of the original farmhouse have remained intact. An authentic, relaxed country atmosphere has been created inside the house, thanks to the tasteful combination of old building materials and rustic antiques.

A hunting trophy (deer antlers) has been transformed into a light. Around the table is a pair of antique Dutch chairs.

During the restoration work all of the interior walls were knocked down, but the atmosphere of yesteryear still prevails: old timber and hand-fired tiles and a tree trunk that has been transformed to make a coffee table.

↖
The entrance hall has been painted with green lime paints. Old terracotta floors have also been laid here.

TRANSFORMATION OF A 200-YEAR-OLD FARMHOUSE INTO A CLASSIC CONTEMPORARY COUNTRY HOME

This farmhouse, which is more than two hundred years old (built in around 1800), idyllically situated in a magnificent natural landscape near Lier (province of Antwerp), has recently been transformed into an authentic country house by interior designer Catherine De Vil. The garden has also been thoroughly redesigned: various terraces and an outdoor swimming pool have been added.

The kitchen offers a view of the scullery and looks out onto the front garden and orchard. Old terracotta floor. The kitchen cupboards were custom made in handscraped pine planks that turn on pivots. Plate rack in aged oak.

The scullery. Washing machine and airing cupboard are concealed behind oak doors. An old bluestone washbasin with a brass tap. The brown tiles are from Emery & Cie. The dark appearance is livened up with some tortoiseshell tiles. Surfaces with concealed oak supports. Work surface with wrought-iron slat and tiles.

↖
The office has been painted in dark-red paints from Emery & Cie. Shelving in painted MDF. Floor in aged, dark-polished oak planks. Cowskin rug. An old wing-chair in the original material. Art by photographer Peter Lindbergh and painter Renaat Ivens (both at Galery Geukens & De Vil).

REHABILITATION

The historic Vaucellehof is situated between Bruges and the North Sea coast.
The abbey and farmhouse complex belonged to the Vaucelle fathers
and includes 17th, 18th and 19th century buildings.
The antiquarian couple Garnier acquired this domain in 1999 and started
the restoration works that have lasted more than ten years.

www.garnier.be

«Os de mouton» settees and an 18th-century walnut parquet flooring.

The guest room with English inspiration: a mahogany 18th century library and antique parquet floor, also in mahogany. Bed linen by Shabby Chic.

↖
The cloakroom cupboards (at the back of the photograph) are made from 19th century antique doors. The stairs are made from oak.

CHATEAU CASTIGNO

A few years ago, the Belgian couple Marc and Tine Verstraete decided to
bring back to life a forgotten wine château in Southern France.
Château Castigno is an exceptional place in Saint-Chinian (near Carcassonne)
with a big ambition: to produce the best wine of Languedoc-Roussillon.
And the domain already seems to have succeeded: Château Castigno's top wines are served
in prestigious star restaurants such as De Karmeliet, Hostellerie Le Fox, Het Gebaar, Hof ter
Eycken, … and their quality and unique characteristics are recognized throughout the world.

www.chateaucastigno.com

Red, purple, rose: these colours refer to the wines produced at the domain, and they also refer to Château Castigno's corporate identity. These colours are repeated everywhere: they also boost extra energy, a very dynamic colour palette in serene surroundings loaded with history.

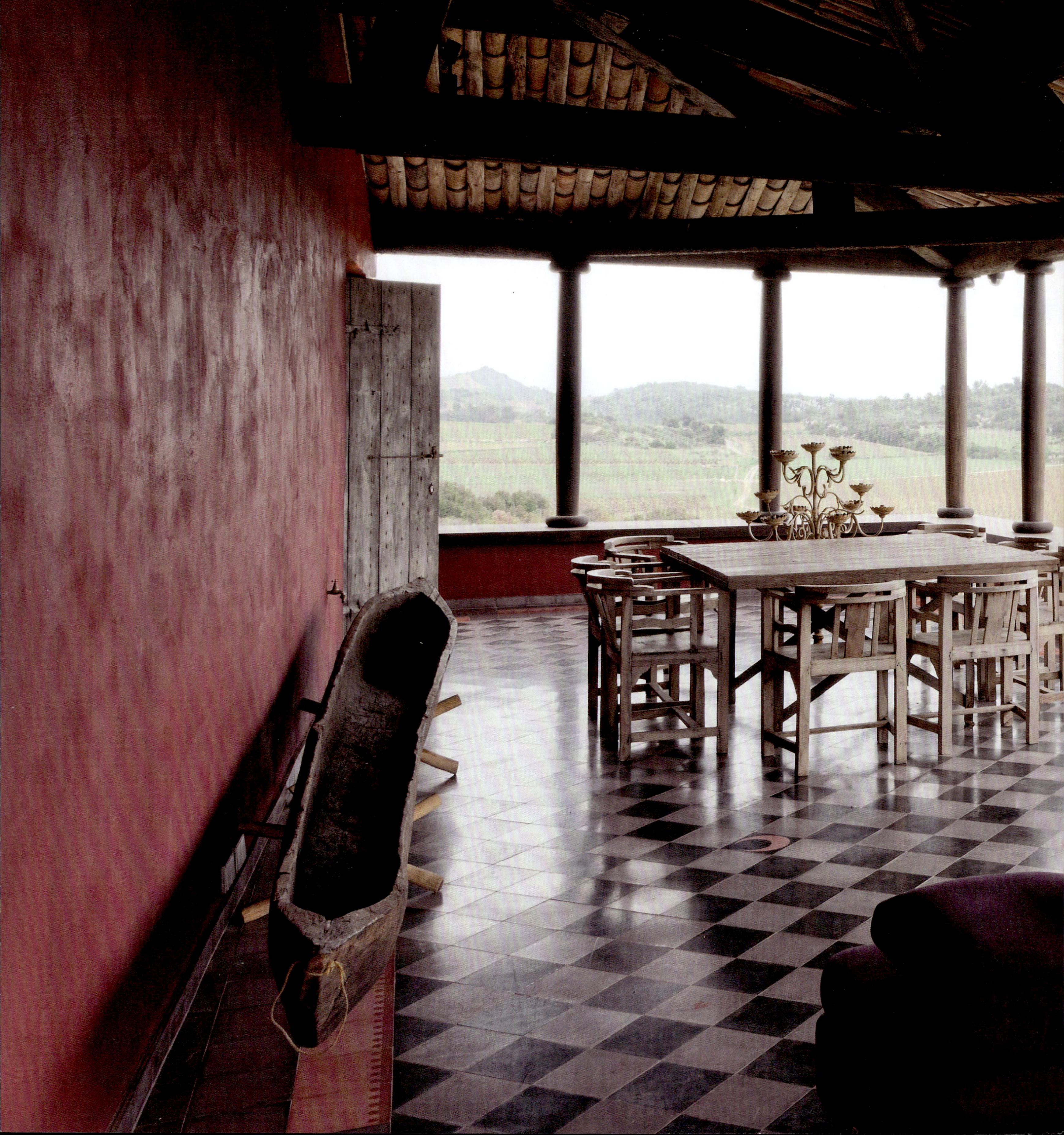

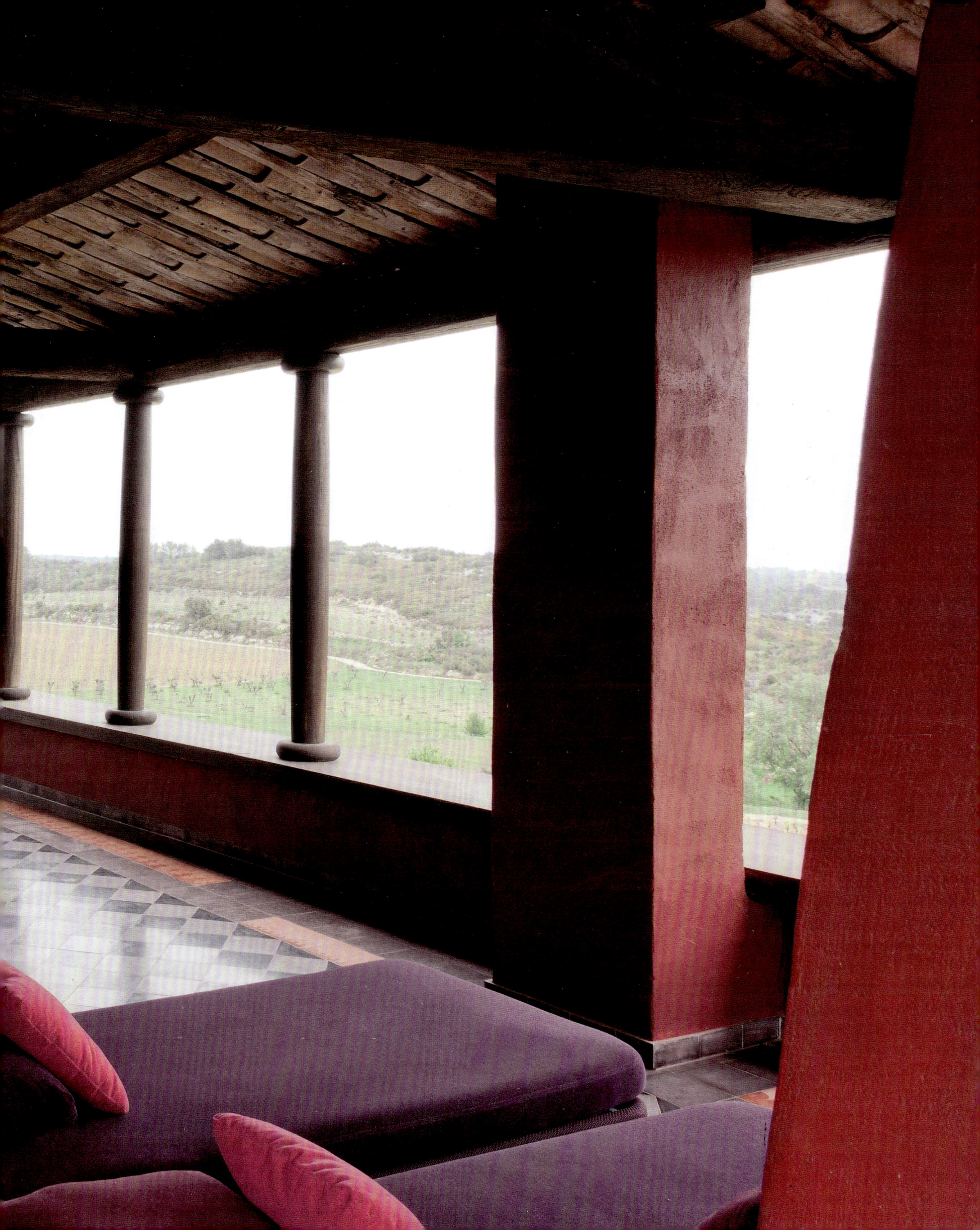

The television room is decorated as a chapel, with two famous works by art photographer David LaChapelle.

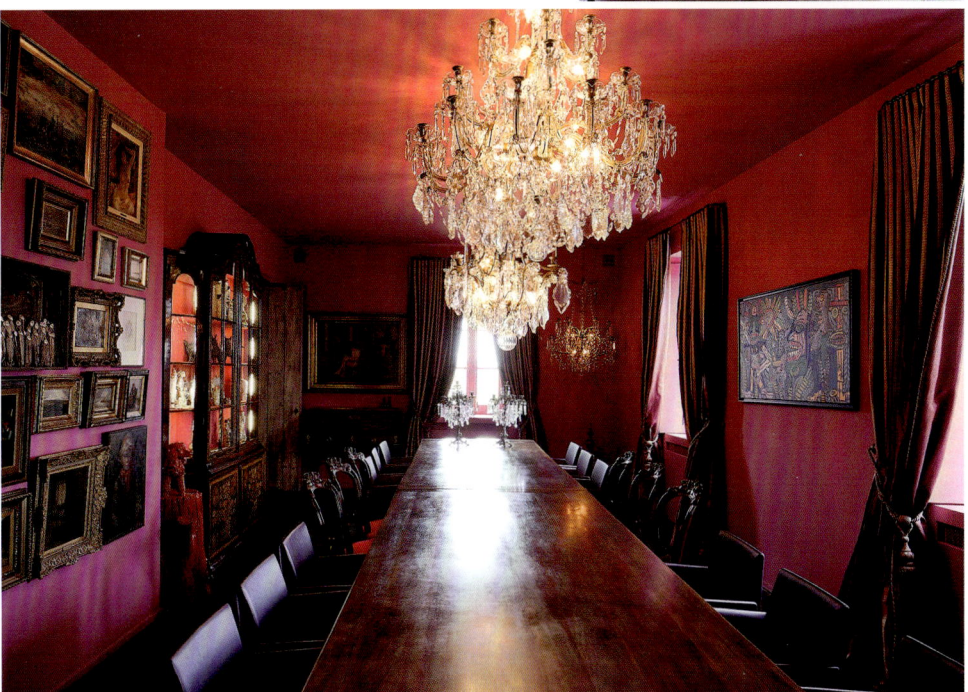

The Knights' Hall, with artefacts from the owners' personal collection.

The television room is decorated as a chapel, with two famous works by art photographer David LaChapelle.

The kitchen is bathing in shades of red and offers a unique view onto the Pyrenees and vineyards.
In the middle, a La Cornue stove, created in cooperation with designer Delvaux for the centenary of this famous Royal Household Purveyor of high-quality culinary pianos. The kitchen cabinets were custom made by Obumex.

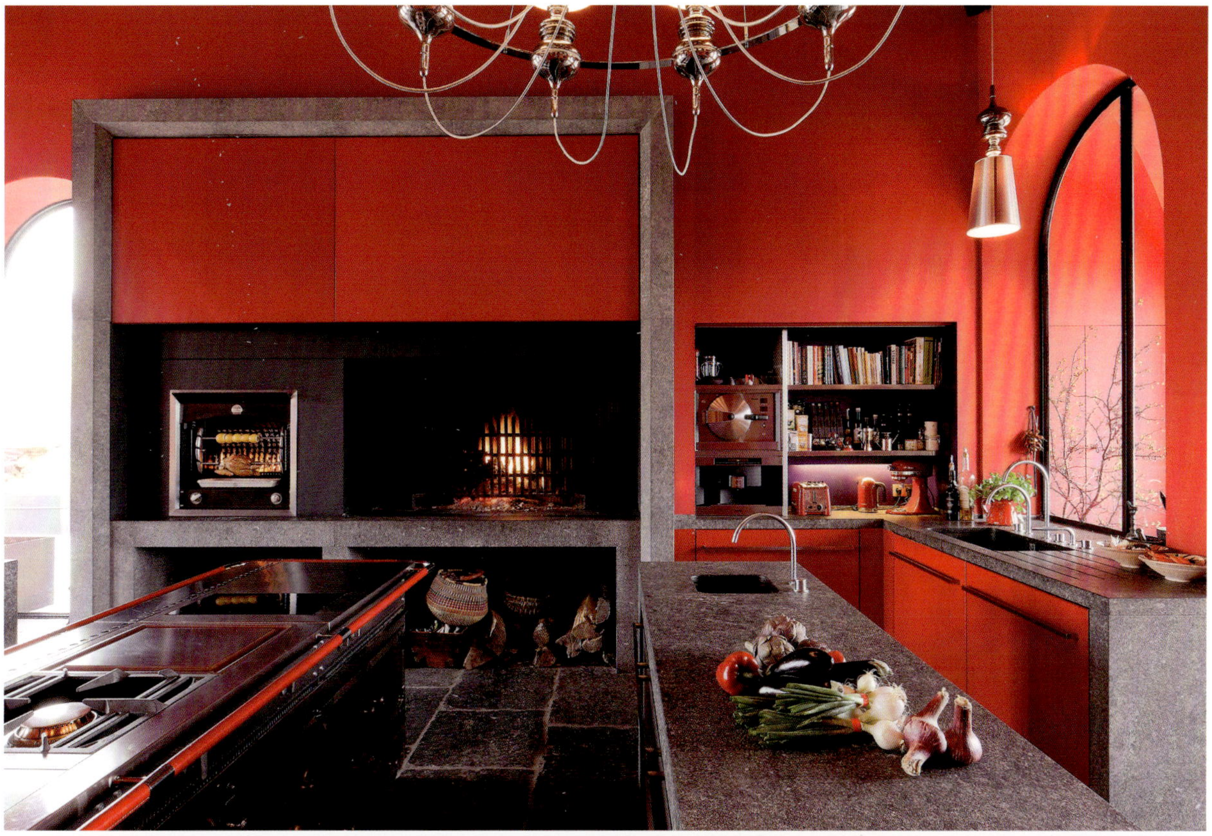

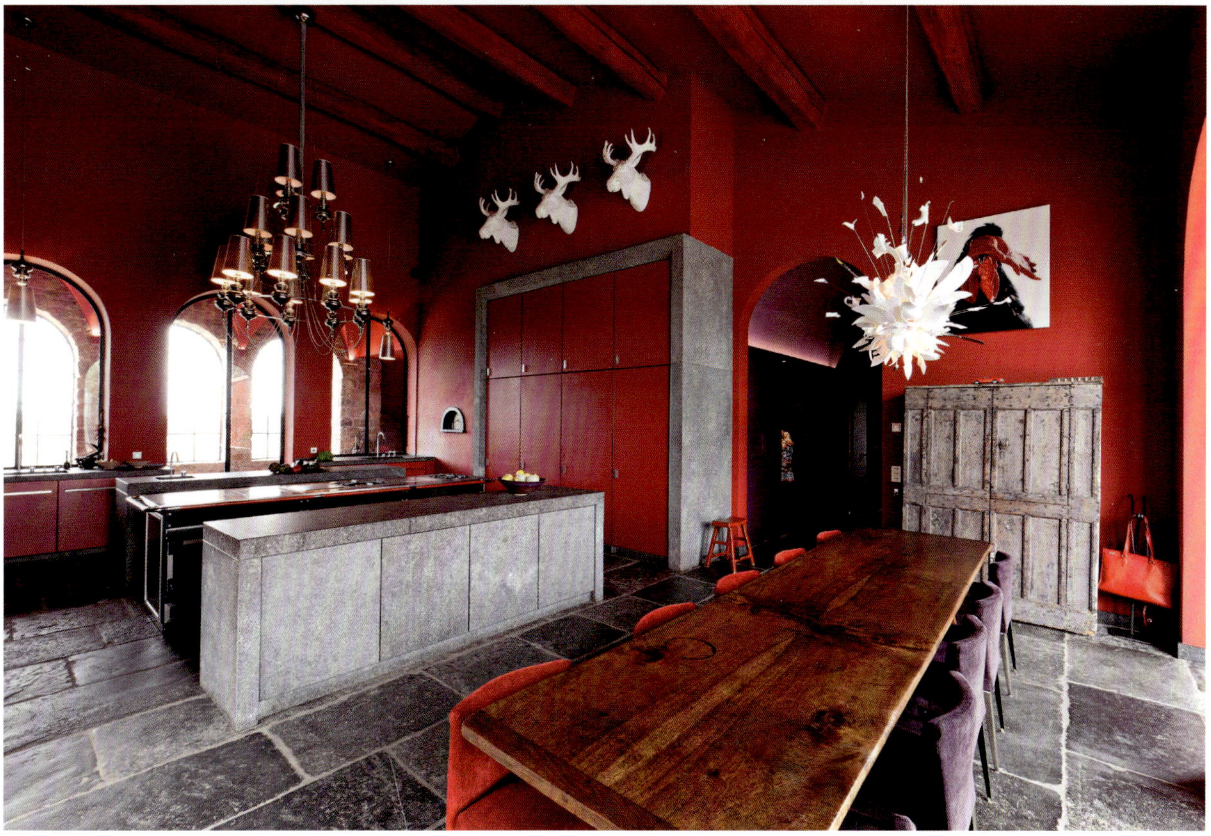

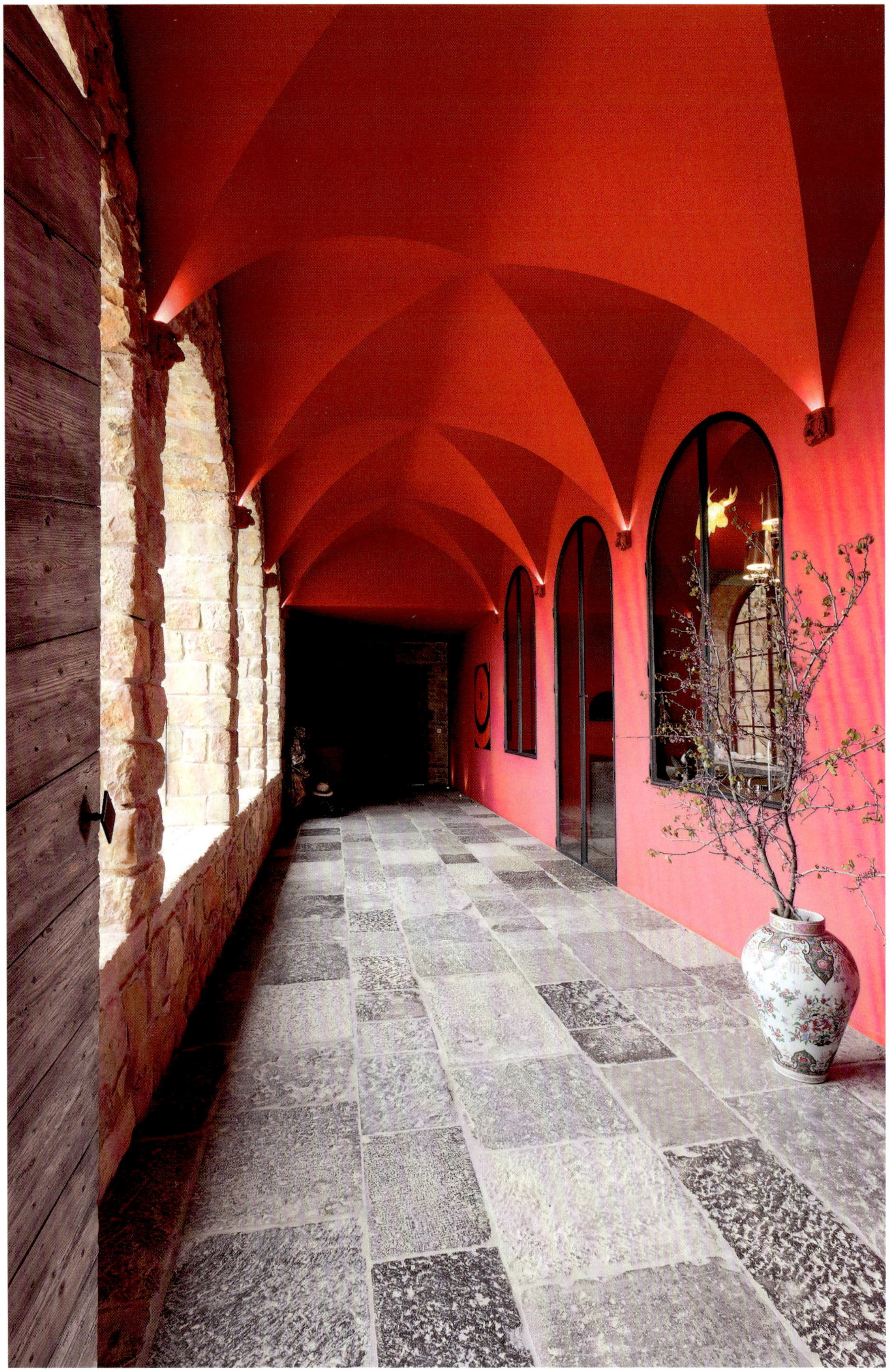

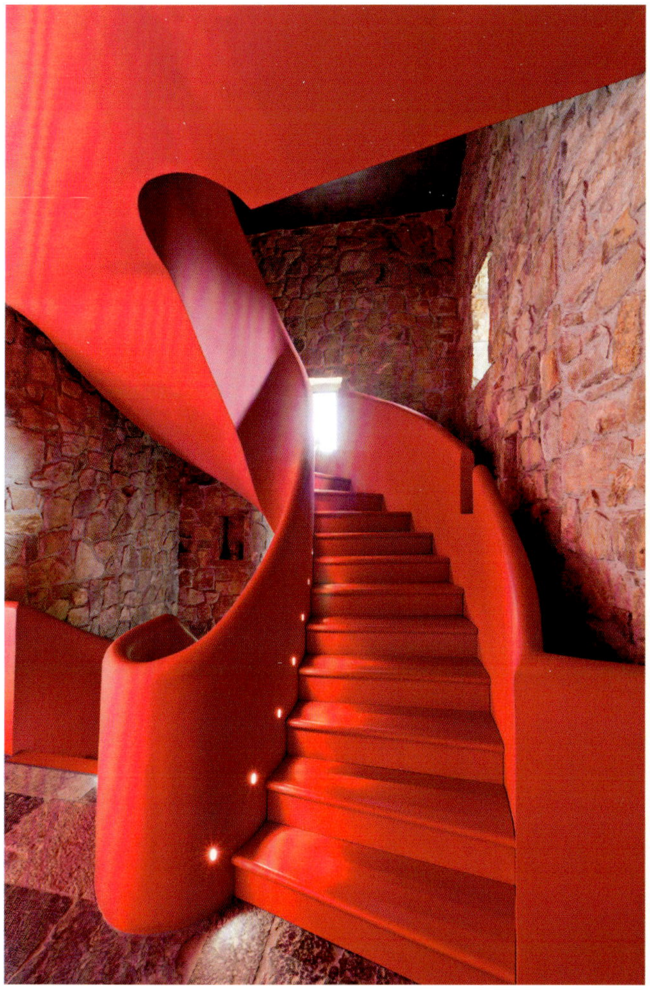
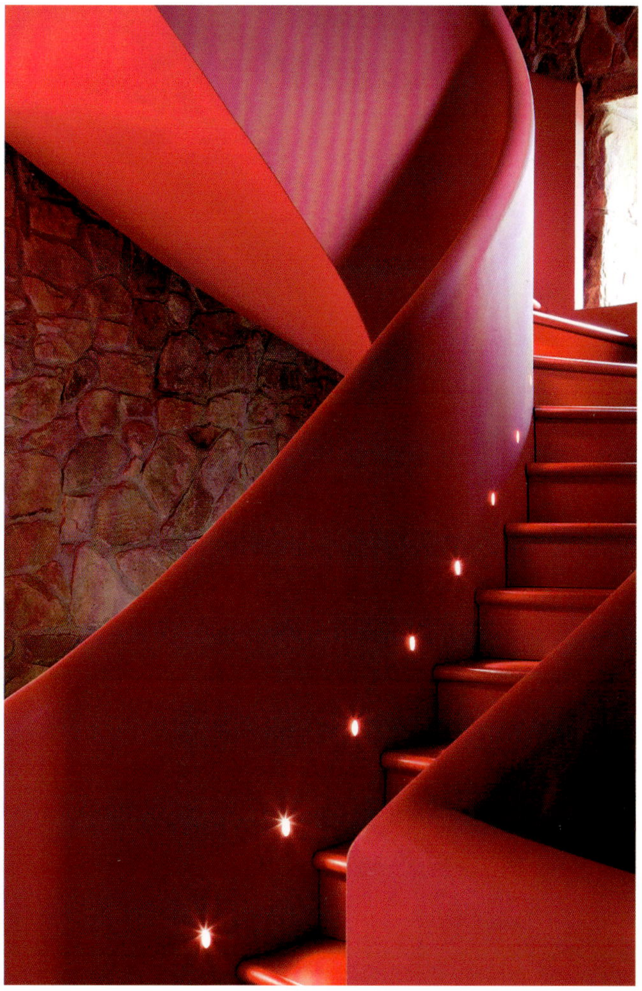

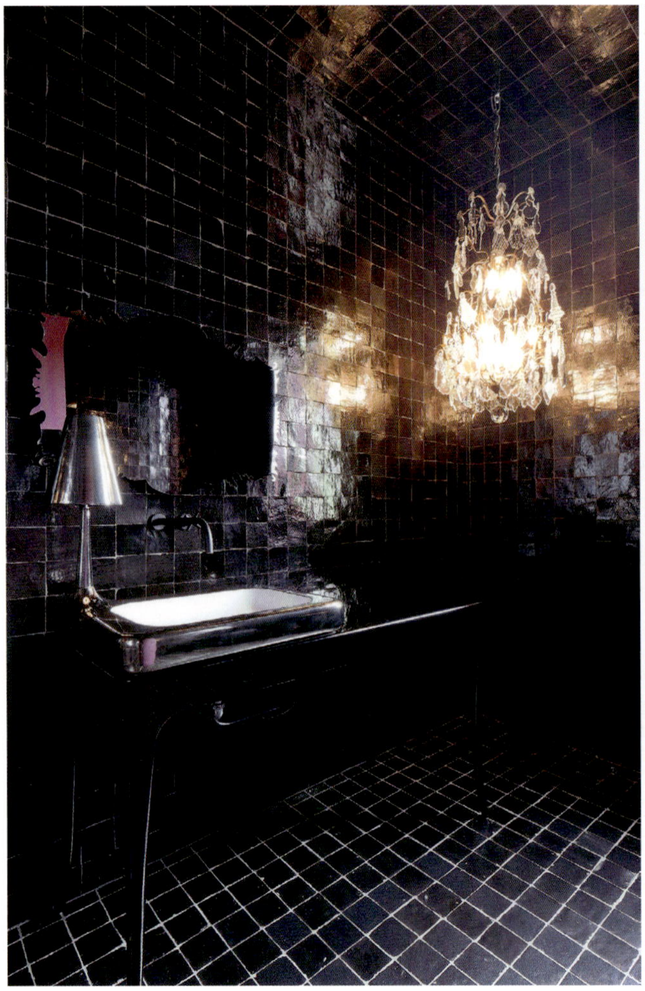

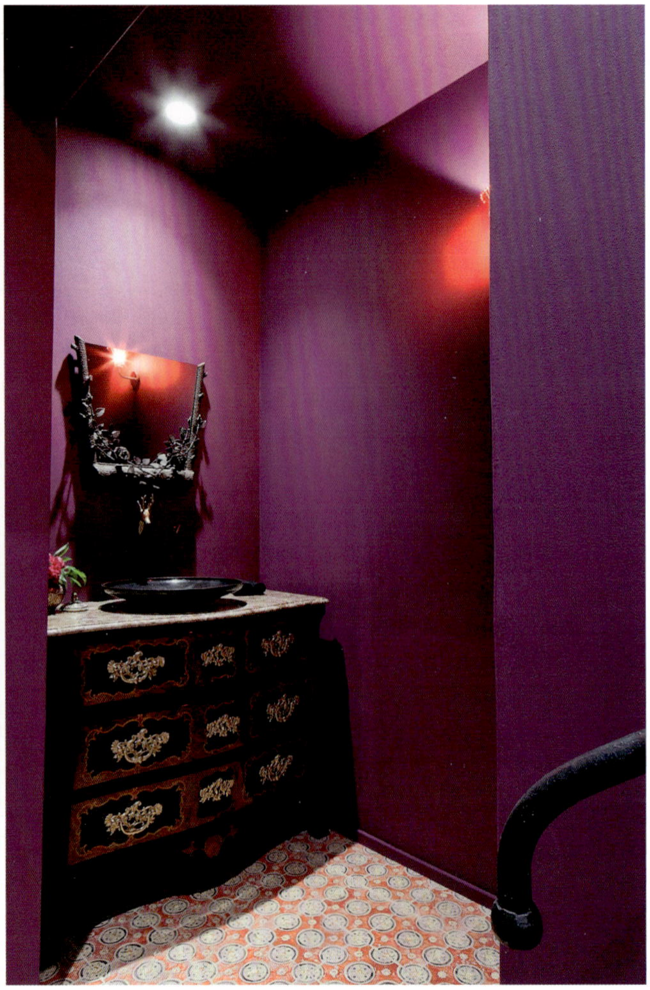

Patrick Ponseele manufactured
the curtains with great skill.

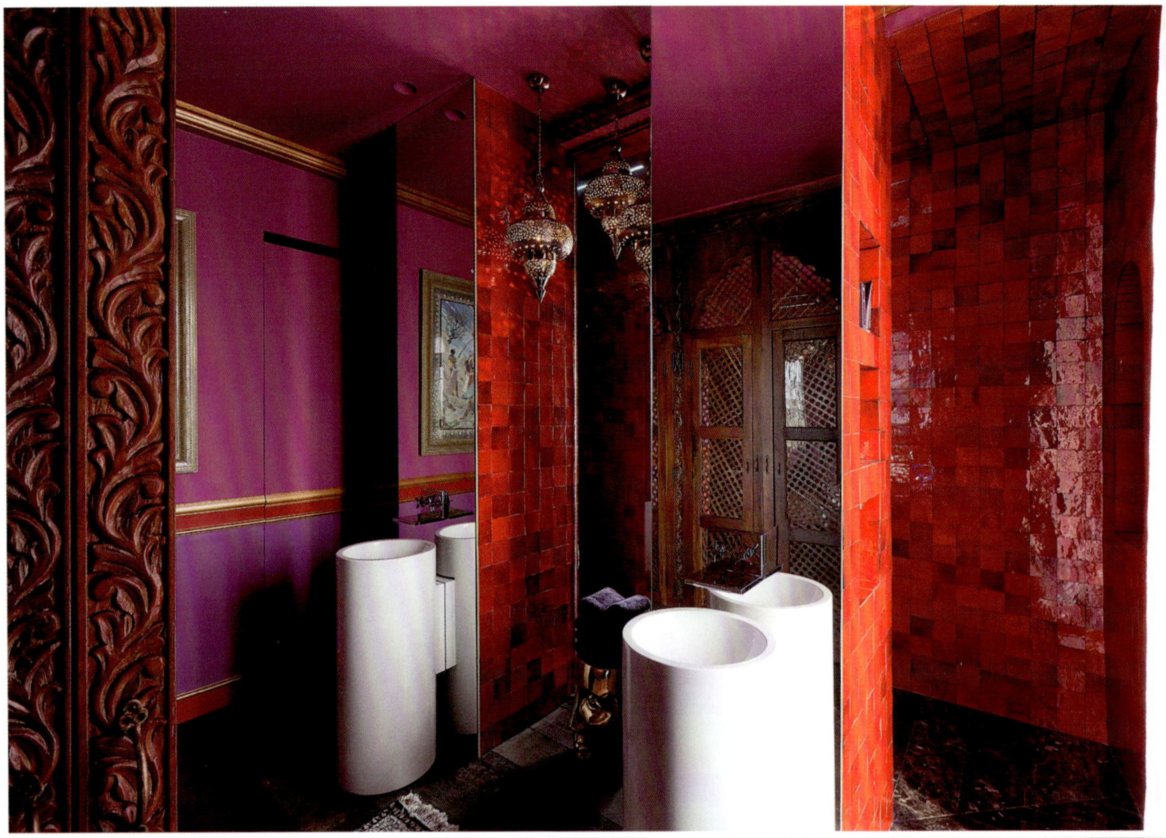

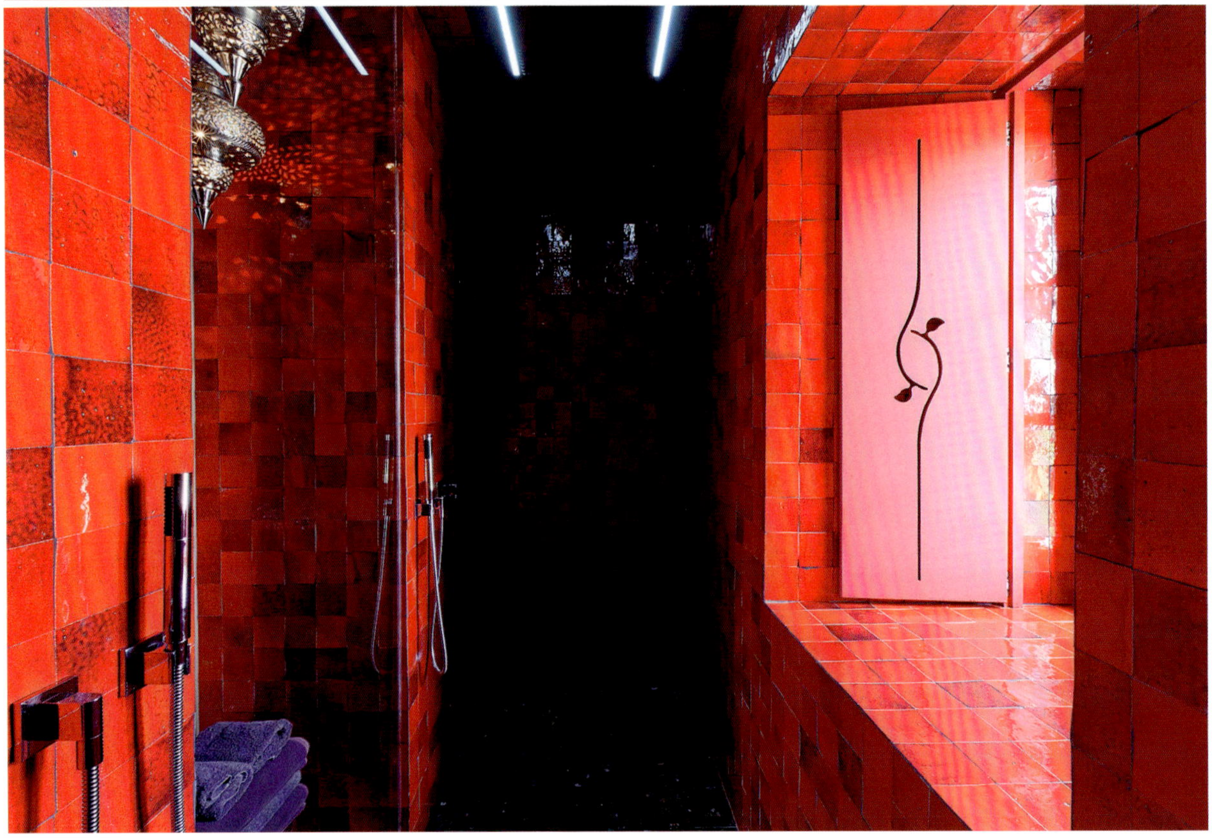

59

A SANCTUARY OF PEACE

This mansion which dates back to 1884 has had very little work done to it over the years. As a result, the original structures and decorative features have been preserved. However, significant restoration work was required and the techniques used to carry out this work needed to be completely revised. The mansion has a relaxing and timeless feel to it. It has become a home-workshop where Anne Derasse has established her offices; the mansion is a veritable sanctuary of peace at the heart of the capital and comprises a house at the front with a garden containing old fruit trees, box trees and pruned hornbeams. There is also a house to the rear which has an old pigeon house.

www.annederasse.be

The atrium window is built into the wall of the rear façade; the wall acts as a support for the vine and was painted completely in anthracite grey right up to the top of the house, whereas the other walls below the atrium have been left in a chalk colour so as to highlight the effect of the shadows and light created by the vine leaves.
Keim exterior mineral paints have been used.
The atrium window establishes a link between the lounge and the garden; in summer, dining under the trellis is possible by virtue of the atrium window.

The motifs in the centre of the ceiling, the borders of the low panelling and the gold plated foliage on the doors are original; they were restored in accordance with industry best practices. In a move away from the tones which already existed in the property, the colour of the moulding and walls have been subtly reworked to reveal tones akin to kaki and sand.
Seigneurie paints have been used to restore the existing paintwork: Rose & Partners. The existing white marble chimney has been preserved. The table is a prototype from the designer S.Lebrun and is made from solid oak which has not been treated and the legs are made from oxidised steel.

↖
The four doors in the lounge located near the atrium window, made originally with an imitation wood finish, have been cleaned and polished.
To maintain the dark colour of the walls, a deep green bronze paint has been applied and the floorboards have been painted in an ebony colour.
The shades of bronze signal the start of a range of colours which will be used again or used in a lighter form in the adjoining dining room.

A COLOURFUL COUNTRY RETREAT

This distinctive country house, built by Renoplan, is a constant source of inspiration for its current owners. The property is conveniently situated close to several major traffic routes, but lies in untouched, idyllic countryside, amongst meadows and woodland. Thanks to the owner's skill and her packed address book, which includes interior decorators Odile and Virginie Dejaegere, antiques dealer Axel Vervoordt, antiques dealers/interior decorators Brigitte and Alain Garnier, landscape architect Anne-Flore Trekels and Hugo Maes' plant nursery, this home has developed an inimitable atmosphere of sophistication over the course of more than ten years.

www.garnier.be   www.axel-vervoordt.com

The bathroom and bedrooms are a fascinating mix of cultural and stylistic influences: luxurious panelling and an Aubusson carpet in the bedroom, an antique bath in solid Carrara marble, warm, Tuscan colours, marble designs and faux marbre painting techniques.

↖
The curtains and tablecloth are in fabrics by Métaphores.

A TIMELESS ENGLISH MANOR

Within a setting of lovely park trees, Costermans Villa Projects realised a timeless English manor. The architectural design and use of materials have strong English roots. Old bricks (baked in open ovens), oak windows, recuperated roof tiles and elegant wrought ironwork melt into a harmonious and timeless whole. The garden architecture was approached in a playful way in order to respect its park-like character as much as possible. When making a stroll through the garden, you will meet a renovated pond surrounded by cobbles from the Meuse River: a closed meander of the nearby brook. When further following the path, you will cross the oak outhouse and parade onwards along some romantic cupids.

www.costermans-projecten.be

A nice dining room is located between living room and kitchen, where one can descend into comfortable armchairs. Axes play an important role in this house; they ensure that the spaces melt into each other nicely. Old whitestone floors continue into the kitchen and scullery.

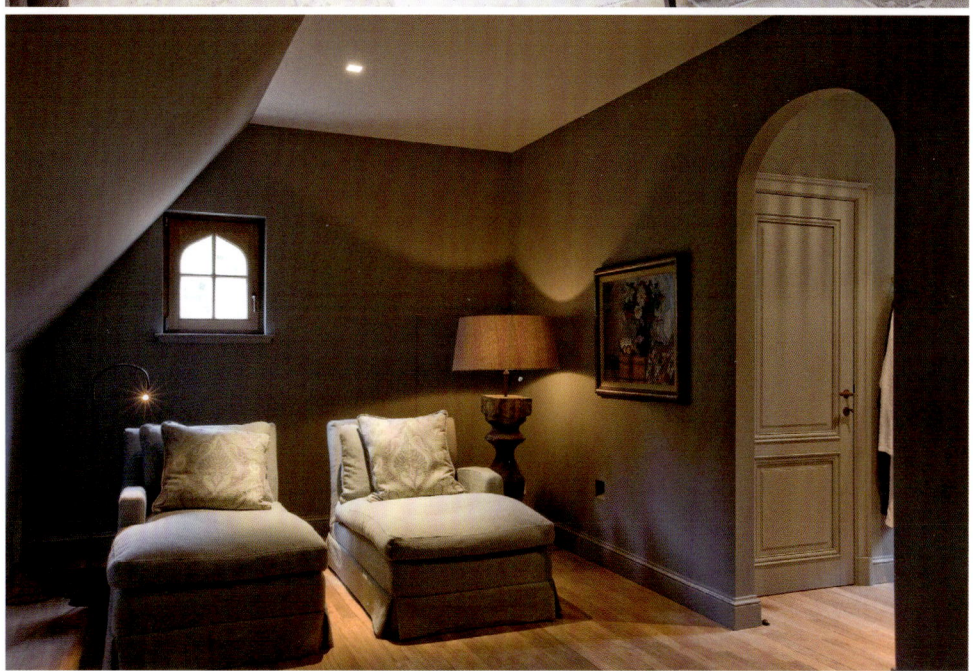

↖
The spacious entrance hall immediately displays the character of the house: a harmonious whole of old materials, oak, wrought ironwork and warm colours. The historic floors form a pattern of whitestone with black slate stoppers. The staircase is in English style with its obliquely mounted wrought-iron balusters. The adjacent office is panelled in oak wainscoting and the fire place creates a comfortable atmosphere. The old plank floor is laid in a ladder structure.

PARIS *PIED-A-TERRE*

This 230 m² apartment in the heart of the 17ᵉ arrondissement in Paris, close to the Parc Monceau, is part of a beautiful property dating from 1910 with backyard. Interior designer Romeo Sozzi, the founder and owner of Promemoria, designs 10 to 15 new pieces of furniture every year adding to his collection. In his Paris apartment, Sozzi displays prototypes, limited editions and unique samples from his collection in a search for perfection, which in no way upset the peace and serenity of this special place in any way. The herringbone parquet floor in oak, beautifully tinted in anthracite grey, is in subtle harmony with the walls in light amethyst decorated with Haussmanian mouldings. One can see the passion for beauty and an eye for detail that have become the trademark of Romeo Sozzi.

www.promemoria.com

A large "Kyoto" kitchen cabinet with sliding glass doors. The fronts are finished in aubergine-coloured varnish with an amethyst-coloured varnish on the inside. Dinnerware from Gien.

The dining room. An oval "Erasmo" table: top in rosewood and a bronze base. "Sofia" chairs in lacquered beechwood and upholstered in velvet.
A "Cecile" reading lamp, a bronze creation with parchment shade and a "Bip Bip" side table with the structure and handle in bronze, a plateau covered in leather and a good-luck frog in Murano glass for Promemoria.

↖
The studio.
On the "Theo" rosewood desk with bronze foot and handles, a "Cecile" reading lamp with bronze structure and a parchment shade.
A "Molly" chair in Mahogany-tinted beech, upholstered in a parma grey taffeta fabric.
The drawing room is on the other side of the doors.

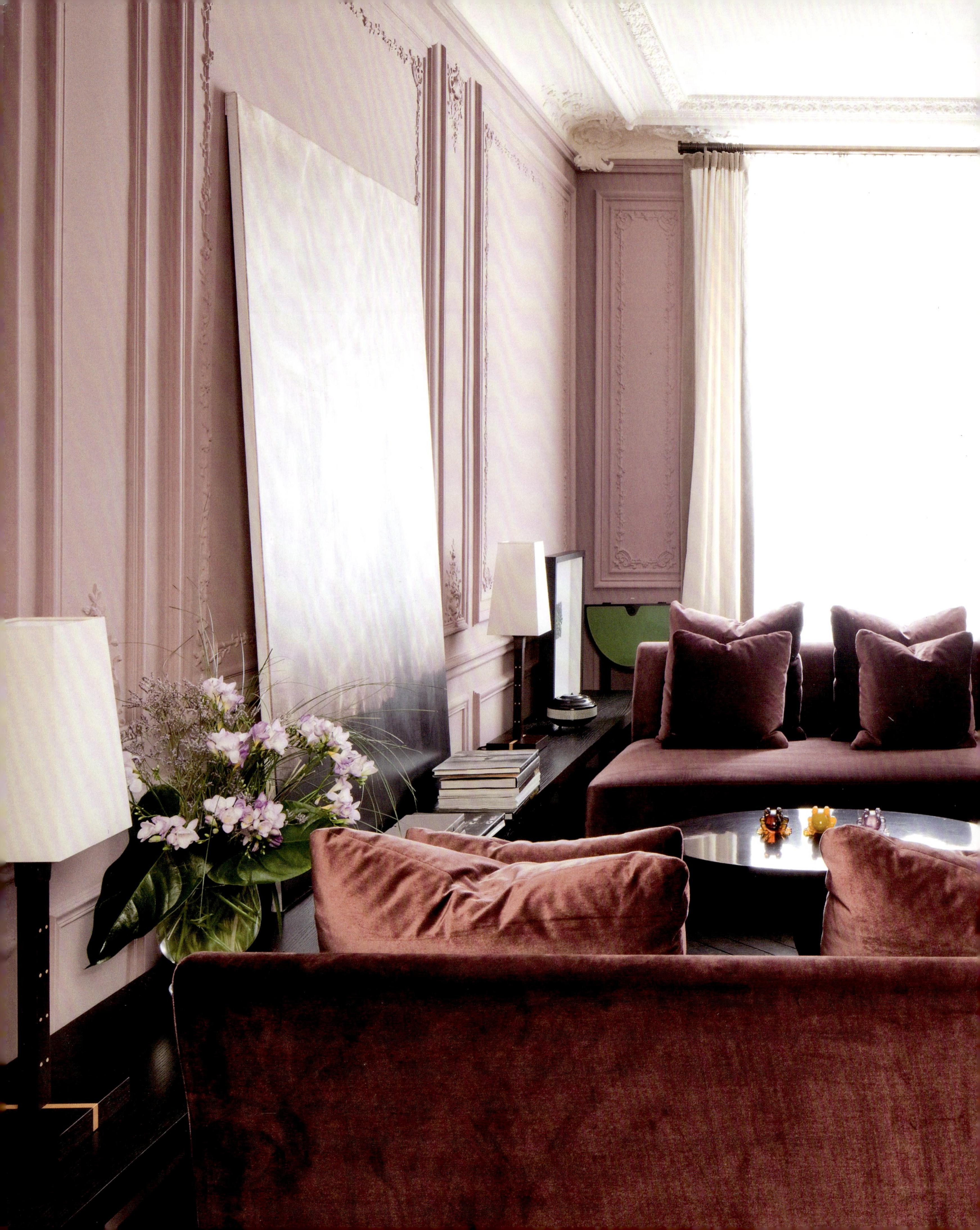

The living room with "Augusto" divans, a "Bassano Gueridon" with ebony and bronze inlays. Hassocks in "Coccolone" velvet and IDA wengé standing lamps.
To the right of the window a "Pia" leather and bronze lampshade, to the left a fold-up "Battista" side table in green leather and black lacquer.

INSPIRED BY AMSTERDAM

Originally Annemarie and Robert wanted renovation plans designed for their house in the green environment of Antwerp. However, Paul Vanrunxt, from the building company Vincent Bruggen, instead suggested to knock down the existing house and to build a house inspired by the Amsterdam canal-side houses. To his own surprise they immediately agreed with this proposition. Annemarie and Robert came to Paul Vanrunxt after a visit in his showhouse in Keerbergen. The clients immediately knew that they wanted to cooperate with Vincent Bruggen. It seemed that the company was specialized in Canadian wood skeleton construction. The owners weren't directly looking for that, but upon hearing more about the principles and advantages of this construction style they were immediately hooked.

www.vincentbruggen.be

The front was designed by Paul Vanrunxt in a very symmetrical way, with a typical gutter and block system windows which were painted with high polished lacquer. This to contrast the black roughcast. The roofing material consists of recycled, blue smoked OVH tiles.

From the kitchen and the sitting corner you can go to a huge roofed terrace with a fireplace.
The windows are also realized by the Atelier Vincent Bruggen.
The garden is signed by Gysel & Stockmans.

From the entrance hall you can go to the office, the playroom, the kitchen and the sitting corner. A painting by Liesbeth Swinnen. The loose accessories mainly come from TS Michielsen De Weijer from Breda.

The massive oak doors reach the ceiling. Kitchen, doors and closets also come from the Atelier Vincent Bruggen.

A DIFFERENT GUESTHOUSE

An oasis of peace, preponderantly classic and a square farm that appeals to the imagination: the trend-setting scenario for this project for which the motivation was to aim for a spotless image. This challenging professional construction project was developed and completed by Wim Beyaert. From now on, everybody can enjoy the accomplishment: the square farm is now used as guest rooms and has been named Le Temps Différent. To carry out this unique project, he consulted Frank Tack, the specialist in quality woodworking from a renowned family business that has been designing and manufacturing the most beautiful kitchens and custom-made furniture for three generations already.

www.franktack.eu

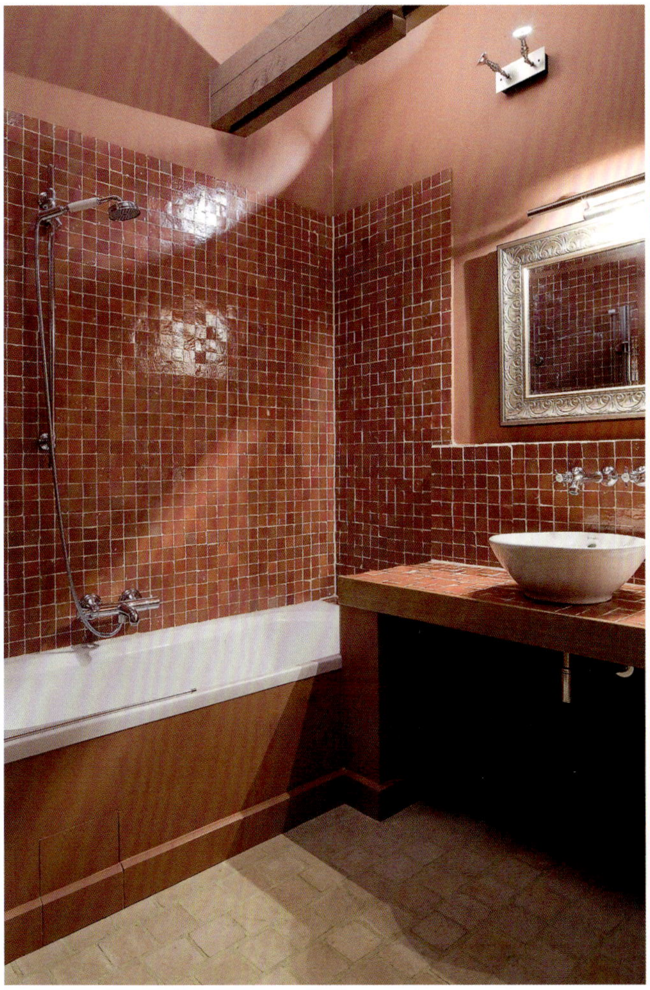

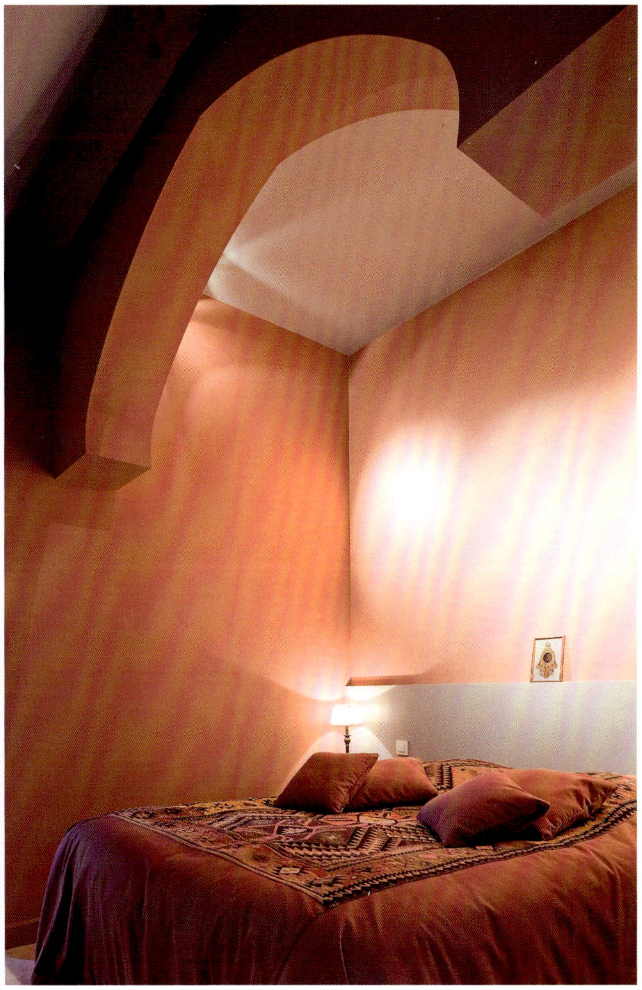

A PERFECT SYMBIOSIS

In this recent Mi Casa realization, the company, specialized in massive wooden construction, shows that the combination with a classical brick construction can equally lead to a perfect symbiosis. This country house, situated near the coast of Knokke, has been designed by the Bureau of Architects E&L Projects. Both outside as well as inside the use of massive wood brings in an extra dimension: a remarkable intimate and warm living environment which provides a permanent sense of holiday.

www.micasa.be

In this drawing room they have opted for a special oak parquet floor in 1x1 m Versailles panels.

A TRIPLEX APARTMENT IN PARIS

Hélène and Olivier Lempereur created authentic charm in an artist's studio over three floors in the heart of the 17th arrondissement in Paris.

www.olivierlempereur.com

The architecture of the kitchen has a strong structure, with light oak in harmony with the zinc and iron furniture.

The bathroom floor is clad with a parquet design in grey natural stone. Horizontal lines in the washbasin and mosaic tiles.

A COUNTRY HOUSE NEAR BRUSSELS

This country house, situated in the green outskirts of Brussels, was built in the 1920s and has recently been renovated for the second time by interior designer Esther Gutmer.

www.esthergutmer.be

Chocolate-brown plastered and polished walls in this boudoir with wall lamps by Ralph Lauren.
The washbasin - an Esther Gutmer design made in veined marble – appears to float between its side supports, which are made of rare wood with a polished finish.

↖
To create a cosy atmosphere in the dining room, Esther Gutmer has chosen warm materials and sober shades such as navy blue and black. Chairs by Ralph Lauren and a Starck chandelier in Baccarat Noir crystal.

A REAL SYMBIOSIS

Stephanie Laporte (The Office) created a contemporary interior for a young family with children in a former presbytery that is a listed building. Architect J.P. Decordier was responsible for the extension and restoration work for the project. After the structural work was completed, the work of the interior architect began. It was of prime importance to create a symbiosis between the old and new parts of the building, whilst retaining the character of the original presbytery. This constant search for the ideal balance resulted in a very special project. Contemporary art was selected for the house in collaboration with Deweer Art Gallery.

www.stephanielaporte.be

The old entrance hall provides a link between the new entrance hall, the dining room and the sitting area. This is a dark and cosy space. The original panelling and the chessboard pattern of the floor harmonise with the piece by Tony Cragg. The coat cupboard is a Laporte design in tinted glass.

↖
The dark shades in the
TV area make this a cosy
space. Koen Vanmechelen's
chickens adorn the wall.

DARK IS BEAUTIFUL

This office is ideally situated on the top floor of an apartment building in the heart of Brussels: a haven of calm in the capital. It is a luxurious and yet also restrained workplace, with fabulous panoramic terraces.

www.ensembleetassocies.be

All the panelling was designed by Ensemble & Associés and finished in sandblasted and black stained larch.

A desk designed by Jean Nouvel for Bulo and desk chairs by Charles Eames.

↖
The library was designed by Ensemble & Associés and finished in sandblasted, black stained larch. A work of art by Mac Cullum.

85

CHEZ ODETTE

As a homage to the owner of a small bistro in the village, the property developer named her new hotel "Chez Odette", a charming guesthouse with six rooms and a refined kitchen. The new hotel proved to be very much to the taste of many city dwellers who visited the village and the decision was taken to design an annex on the other side of the square… Two rooms, a suite and a conference room, a bar and a sitting room, all designed by Ensemble & Associés in close cooperation with the property developer.

www.ensembleetassocies.be

The living room / library with a sofa and armchairs from Flexform in weathered leather. A coffee table in stained cedar and lighting from Pierre Frey.
A composition of old village views on the wall in the form of a hologram and realised by Matthew Andrews.

Library bookshelves designed by Ensemble & Associés and finished in stained oak.

↖
The hotel sitting room.
Armchairs and coffee tables were found by the property developer. A Flexform sofa in weathered leather.

RENOVATION OF A HISTORIC FINCA

La Carrascosa, a historic finca near Jerez de la Frontera (southern Spain), is situated on the foothills of a wild and untouched scenic area that stretches for around eighty kilometres along the Bay of Cadiz, almost as far as the rock of Gibraltar. The owner, a well-travelled businessman, wanted to create a property that would be easy to use in the warm summer months as well as the sometimes unpredictable winter period, for board meetings as well as for holidays and hunting. Christine Bekaert transformed the existing buildings, which had previously been closed, into pleasant winter rooms by using warm colours and materials and by integrating many hunting accessories.

The old hand-knotted woollen carpet comes from the Aït Ouarain tribe of the Central Atlas mountains. The moucharabieh table was made to order in the souk of Marrakech.

Gazelle-skin cushions on the bed. Hand-woven voile brought from Istanbul. A Chinese case in beige leather and an African Ashanti seat. Lamp base made from oyster sticks. Limewash finish on the walls carried out by Kordekor, under the direction of Christine Bekaert.

THE CONTEMPORARY RENOVATION
OF A FORMER HUNTING LODGE

In the green countryside outside Bruges, in the middle of a 150-hectare nature reserve, interior architect Ann Gryp has renovated this former hunting lodge as her own home. The transformation of the country house was a radical one: almost everything was altered. The final result is sober and contemporary with a warm touch.

With the exception of the office, the ground floor is completely open: the kitchen, dining room and living room all run into each other. The flooring downstairs is the same throughout, accentuating the connection between the different spaces. The colours and materials used by Ann Gryp create an atmosphere of warmth and calm.

↖
There is no entrance hall.
The front door opens directly into the dining room.
The front door and windows are integrated into the wall of shelves.

A BLEND OF TIMELESS AND CONTEMPORARY:
A BALANCED PHILOSOPHY FOR LIVING

This farmhouse was created by architect Stéphane Boens.
The owners also use the house as a showroom for am projects, their interior-design company.
Their work is more a philosophy of life than simply decoration.
They create timeless environments and living spaces that are perfectly in balance
with the lifestyle of their clients. They decorated this house themselves.

www.stephaneboens.be   www.amprojects.be

The seats in the TV and audio room are in basic linen and can be made to order. Ceiling and panels created by am projects. The designers have ensured that the paintwork and the window decoration form a whole.

THE REVIVAL OF A 19TH-CENTURY CASTLE

This distinctive castle, which was used as a country seat by different generations of noble families, underwent a painstaking restoration a few years ago. The nineteenth-century castle, situated on an estate of five hectares with ancient trees and a variety of ponds in an English landscape style, was bombed during World War I and rebuilt after the war. The present owners restored their historic home in close collaboration with architect Stéphane Boens.

www.stephaneboens.be

↖
All of the fireplaces on each
of the three floors have been
retained.

A STATELY COUNTRY VILLA NEAR ANTWERP

This renovation project in the green environs around Antwerp was entrusted to Sphere Concepts from Schilde. They contacted architect Gerd Van Zundert (AID-Architecten) to adapt the outer walls and to bring these into the correct proportions, after Sphere Concepts had designed the interior layout. The previous layout of the villa was dated, and Sphere Concepts replaced this with an interior that radiates charm, and in particular peace and quiet. Axes and through-views were incorporated where possible, the right materials were chosen, and all colours and finishing trims were decided on with a view to achieving a harmonious and balanced end result. The renovation work was meticulously carried out by the PDK building firm in Deurne.

www.sphereconcepts.be

The custom-made dining-room table is a design of Piet Boon. Above it, a chandelier with candles in Swarovski crystal. The chairs are by Meridiani (Cruz tre model). A hand-tufted carpet in bamboo and silk. Steel glass partitions separate the living room from the dining room and the kitchen.

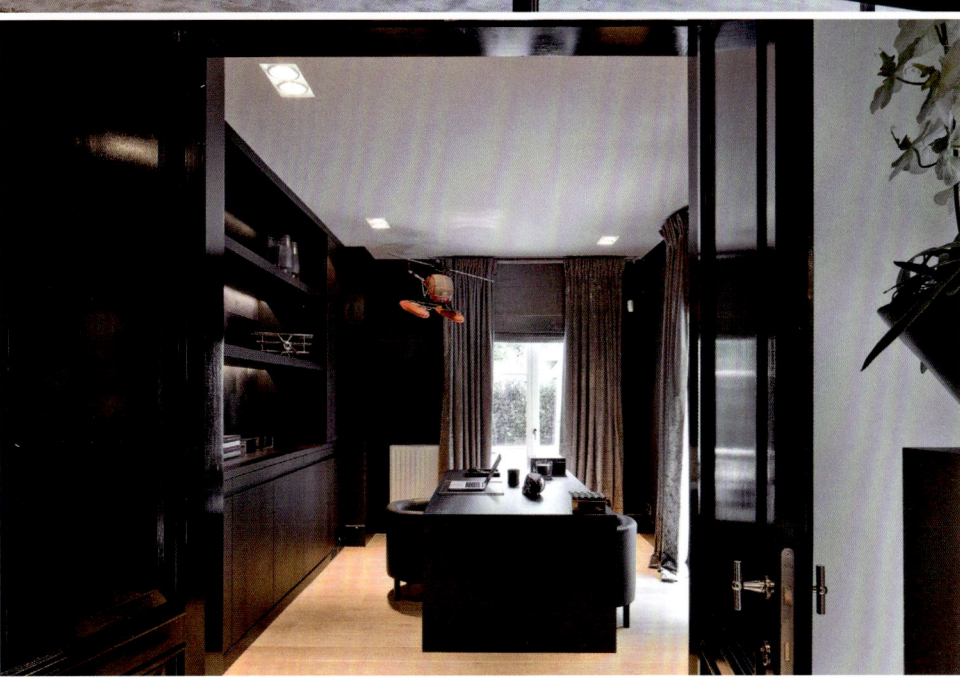

A desk in wenge-stained solid oak. Curtains from Romo in velour.

↖
The living room with an open gas-fired fireplace, a wenge-stained oak chest of drawers with indirect lighting and rear walls clad in a fur wall covering.

97

A VERY TASTEFUL B&B

The owners discovered this farmhouse on an overcast day in May. It was not an obvious choice as somewhere to go and live, but they dreamed of life in the country and saw nothing but prospects in the farmhouse's dilapidated state. When the restoration was carried out, the conscious decision was taken to go for a contemporary approach, involving all the materials being cleaned up and all mod cons being incorporated. Integrating the surrounding landscape into the residence as much as possible was one of the explicit tasks facing architect Gerd Van Zundert, who has succeeded extremely well in doing just that.

www.moka-projects.com   www.moka-vanille.com

Sufficient storage space is vitally important for you to feel comfortable. A shoe cupboard and various store cupboards are concealed behind the poplar partition.

For the guest room in the annexe, a light-pink background was used, which lends itself perfectly to combination with timeless Italian bed linen (everything from Moka Projects).
The black-grey facing of the walk-in shower in tadelakt forms a daring yet warm contrast with the light-pink shades used elsewhere in this room.

↖
The sitting area in the guest accommodation is a very functional room. The dark colours, simple joinery and natural soft furnishings (all from the owner's own workshop) create an intimate atmosphere.

ANGLO-SAXON INSPIRATION

Ilse De Meulemeester created this residence in close cooperation with villa builder Elbeko from Zele and the architects' firm of engineer and architect Bart François in Ghent. The assignment seemed simple: to design a timeless country house with the historical impact of a traditional English cottage, which would be a beacon of peace and quiet and a place with a permanent holiday feel to it.

www.ilsedemeulemeester.be   www.bartfrancois.be

Decorator Ilse De Meulemeester likes to work with a few strong touches of colour. The drawing room exudes restfulness and grandeur, with sofas in black velvet around the fireplace. The mirrored cupboard replete with silverwork (behind the piano) makes this room feel even bigger.

A COSY AND SOBER APARTMENT IN A 17TH-CENTURY LISTED BUILDING

This magnificent 80m² apartment is the result of a collaboration between two interior architects: designer John-Paul Welton and Brigitte Boiron, who is also a project developer. There is nothing to suggest that a gem of contemporary living lies behind the facade of this listed seventeenth-century building in the historic centre of Geneva with a view of St. Pierre Cathedral: a cosy and yet sober, streamlined apartment. The secret of this exceptional place: the inspired choice of furniture, colours and materials.

www.weltondesign.com

The floor and walls of the bathroom and toilet are in polished concrete.
Taps and shower by Ottone Meloda, Aspara collection, model: Riquardi.

↖
A parquet floor in solid wengé and a lacquered wall. A Firenze bed with Lorca fabric from Osborne & Little (at Welton Design). The dressing room was created by cabinetmaker Luc Obersson.
Night lights: Lampe Casa.

A SUBTLE COLOUR PALETTE

For over a decade, Edouard Vermeulen (Natan), the renowned couturier, has lived on the Rozenhout estate: an eighteenth-century country house, or "gentilhommière", situated in glorious parkland. In close collaboration with the architect Raymond Rombouts, the original house was improved and a pavilion added. Edouard Vermeulen – himself an interior designer before he made his name in the world of haute couture – took care of the interior decoration: a timeless and subtle colour palette, in the same spirit as his exclusive collections.

An intimate guest room, painted with lime paints by Dankers Decor. The commode is by Torus.

↖
An impression of the reading room. The couch is from Axel Vervoordt.

RENOVATION OF A TYPICAL FLEMISH COUNTRY HOUSE

Around 1950, a typically Flemish country house was built nearby the royal estate of Bouchout.. In the nineteen-eighties, the house came into the hands of an enthusiastic couple with young children. A top-to-bottom transformation of the property began immediately. The exterior and the architectural layout of the house remained intact, but, under the direction of Axel Vervoordt, the interior decoration was thoroughly revamped. New life was blown into the whole building, which was also restructured and laid out differently. Vervoordt's contribution was invaluable: he taught the lady of the house a great deal about how to beautify and bring life into a home. The owners also took advice from the interior designer Catherine De Vil, who designed the kitchen and the children's bedrooms. Jacques Wirtz redesigned the garden.

A bathroom in Belgian Rouge Royal stone; walls painted with a "trompe-l'oeil" design.

An arch from Vervoordt (on the right) served as a starting point for the furnishing of this room.

↖
The kitchen was designed in collaboration with interior designer Catherine De Vil. The floor is made of old oak planks. The custom-made cupboards have been patinated.

A NEW LIFE

A country house located at the border of two Southern Tuscany valleys (Val d'Orcia and Valdichiana) and abandoned for many years, was discovered by its present owner in the late 90's. With the support of interior decorator Paola Navone and landscape architect Peter Curzon and with a lot of love and patience, he transformed it into his permanent residence. Formerly a fashion industry executive, he now enjoys his new farmer's life, producing wine and olive oil.

The ground floor guest suite with a silver grapes decoration on the light grey walls.

Greek peasants' sheets cover a chair and a day-bed in the "blue guest suite".

↖
Two huge cupboards from Southern France in the main living room.

A JOYFUL FAMILY HOME

This 220 m² family home was designed by the architect Bruno Vanbesien.
The original home offered little light, had no contact with the garden,
was lacking in comfort and situated on a bizarre piece of land.

www.brunovanbesien.be

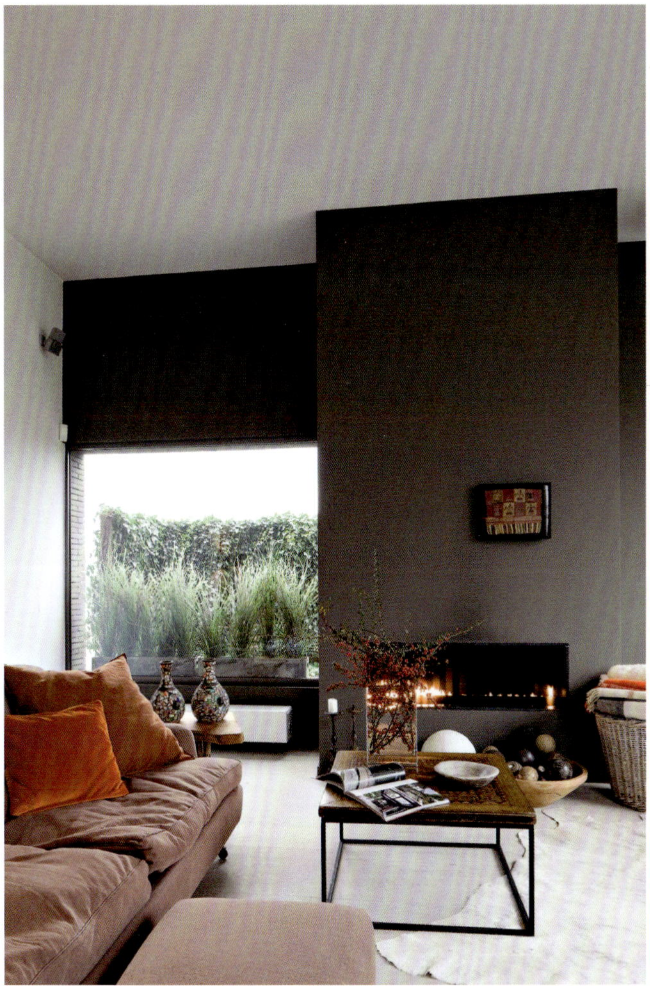

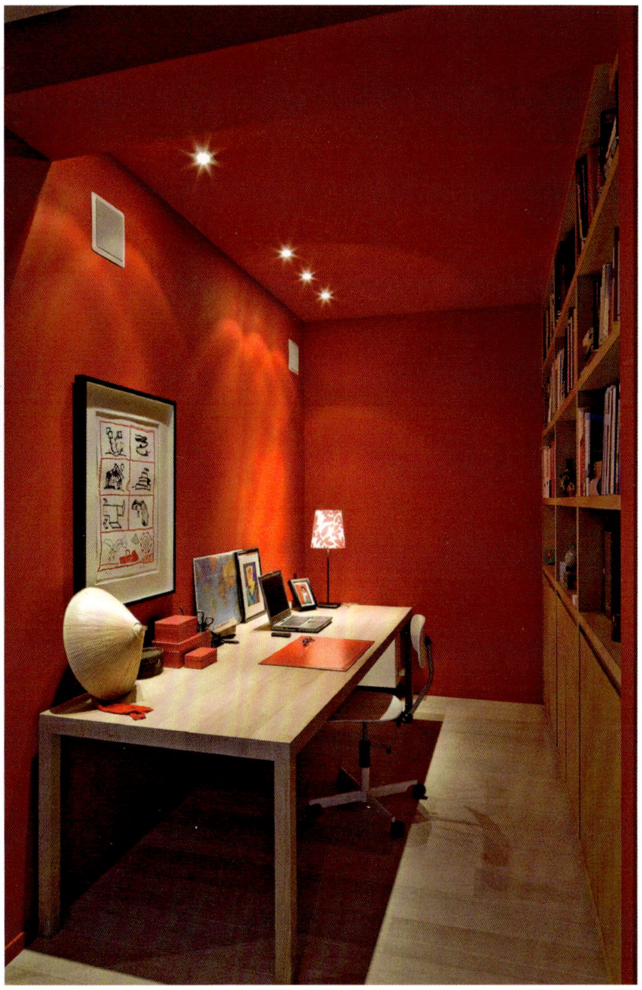

AN APARTMENT IN GENEVA

Interior Architects Brigitte Boiron and John-Paul Welton continue their cooperation further and provide the complete renovation of this apartment of 320 m² located in a historic building in Geneva. They created a timeless and luxurious universe that will honour their art collection, a wish of the residents. The company Project Design was responsible for the complete renewal of the rooms. Under the leadership of Brigitte Boiron the decoration became a perfect blend of the many works of art and the custom-made furniture. John-Paul Welton shows his expertise: the creation and implementation of a part of the furniture, autographed by Welton Design. Knowledge of materials, subtlety of tone on tone colours and the grey tints provide a refined and warm living environment.

www.weltondesign.com

The sofas were custom made. Balthus chaises longues (Casablanca), a Daninos "Bulle" armchair (an original from 1968), Cecile lamps by Promemoria in hammered bronze and a lead statue (5 persons) by Rita Jordens.
A lacquered coffee table by Welton Design. A Stepevi carpet in wool and silk. The acrobat in chromium-plated bronze is by Mauro Corda; the ostrich sculpture (a unique piece of cut aluminium) is by Cipre.

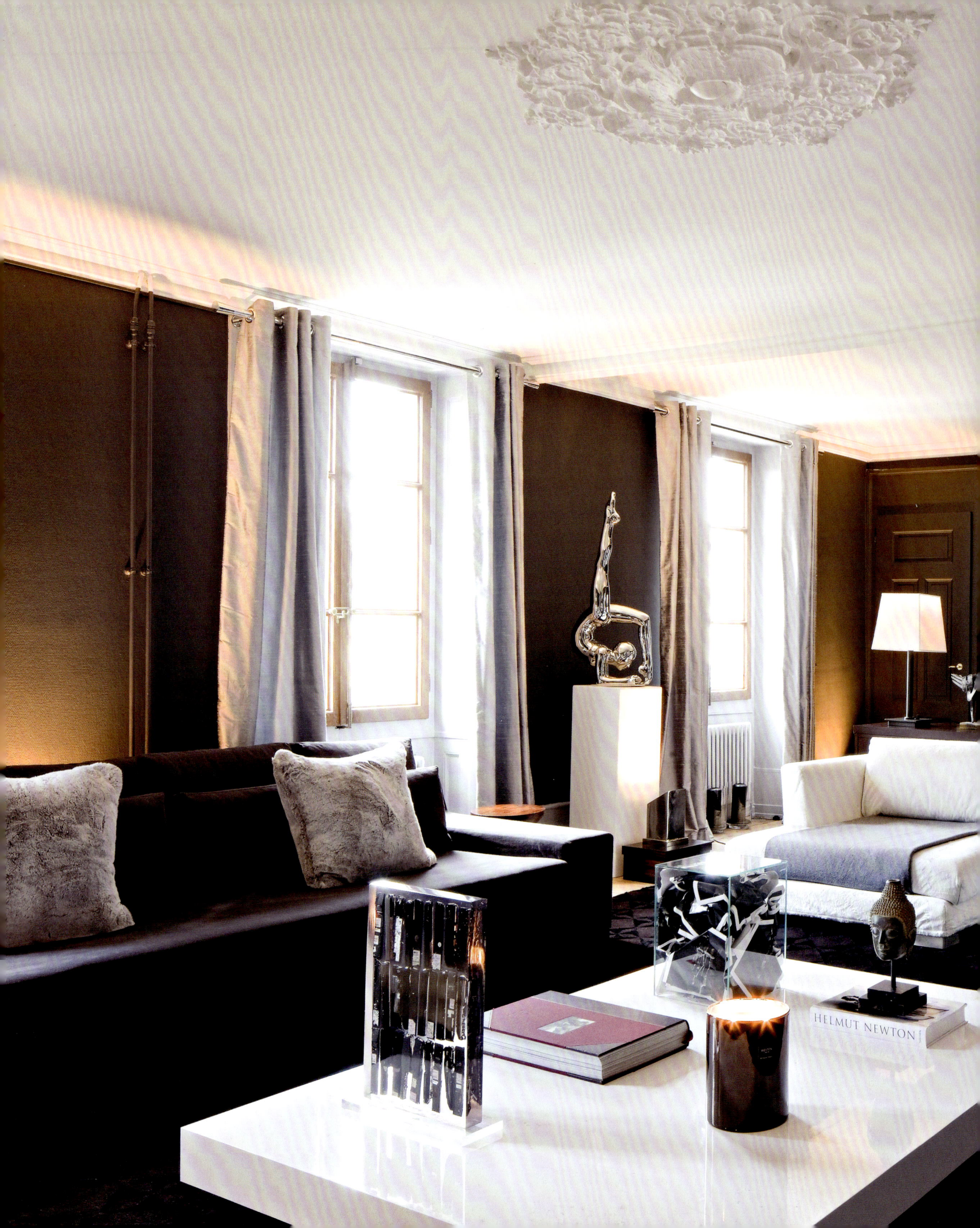
HELMUT NEWTON

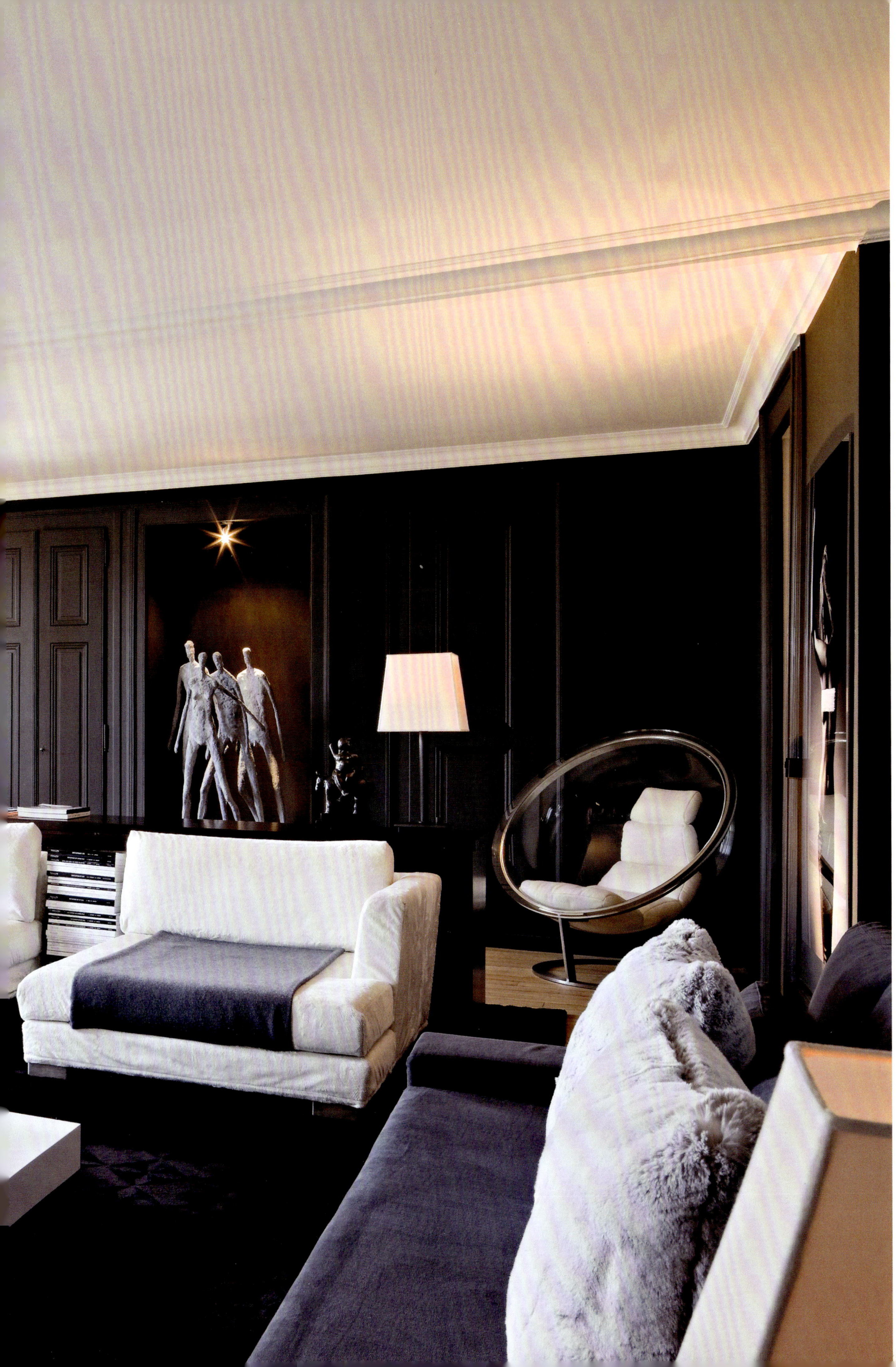

COSMOPOLITAN FEELING

This complete structure was designed by interior architect Nathalie Deboel in collaboration with Obumex. In consultation with the client Obumex chose for the ground floor: a fully customised and personalised interior, where the client can find complete peace and harmony. The consistent use of dark tinted Spanish oak and bronze gives the interior a warm atmosphere. This allows the contemporary artworks to come perfectly into their own. The combination of a timeless and elegant interior with art and antique results in a cosmopolitan whole.

www.obumex.be   www.nathaliedeboel.be

Mosaic by Dominique
Desimpel. The custom-made
sinks were completely covered
with hand cut mosaic.

↖
The lights are by the Belgian
designer Jules Wabbes.

A HOUSE IN THE LUXEMBOURG COUNTRYSIDE

This house was built in 2007 and is situated in the Luxembourg countryside. The interior combines both neutral and timeless elements with some antiques, using natural and noble materials. The house is also used as a show-room for the owners' interior design and decoration business: In Tempo by Luc Leroi. Their philosophy lies in the creation of timeless interiors favouring materials such as natural wood, stone, lime, linen and an overarching use of artisanal work.

www.intempo.lu

The office has an antique pine table and an 18th century "Os de mouton" chair. Lighting from S.Davidts.

Pantry. The storage units have been custom-made. Underfoot, checkerboard flooring in Italian marble by Dominique Desimpel.

↖
The kitchen is in untreated oak, with a work top in blue stone and credenza covered in red zellige tiles from Dominique Desimpel. Integrated storage cabinet and fridge in a cupboard painted the same colour as the wall.

A COUNTRY HOUSE IN THE KEMPEN WOODLAND

Dankers Decor is one of the most important painting companies in the Benelux, with contracts in New York, USA, Hong Kong, the United Arab Emirates, etc. Eddy Dankers, business manager of the company, works closely together with the renowned antiquarian Axel Vervoordt on a lot of projects: for instance he realized all the paintwork in the Chateau of 's-Gravenwezel and Kanaal, both of Axel Vervoordt. A lot of colours and pigments were created especially for the antiquarian. Axel Vervoordt also advised Eddy Dankers for the interior of his own home in the Kempen. This report illustrates the result of their constant search for perfection, not only in the use of colours and painting techniques (e.g. with Corical paints from Arte Constructo), but also in the choice of antique objects and furniture (from Axel Vervoordt) and the soft furnishings with fabrics from Vera Dankers (Dankers Creation).

www.dankers.be

In the night landing there is an exceptional sculpture from the antiquarian Vervoordt. The curtain decoration was provided by Dankers Creation, the company of Vera Dankers. All the walls were finished in lime based paints.

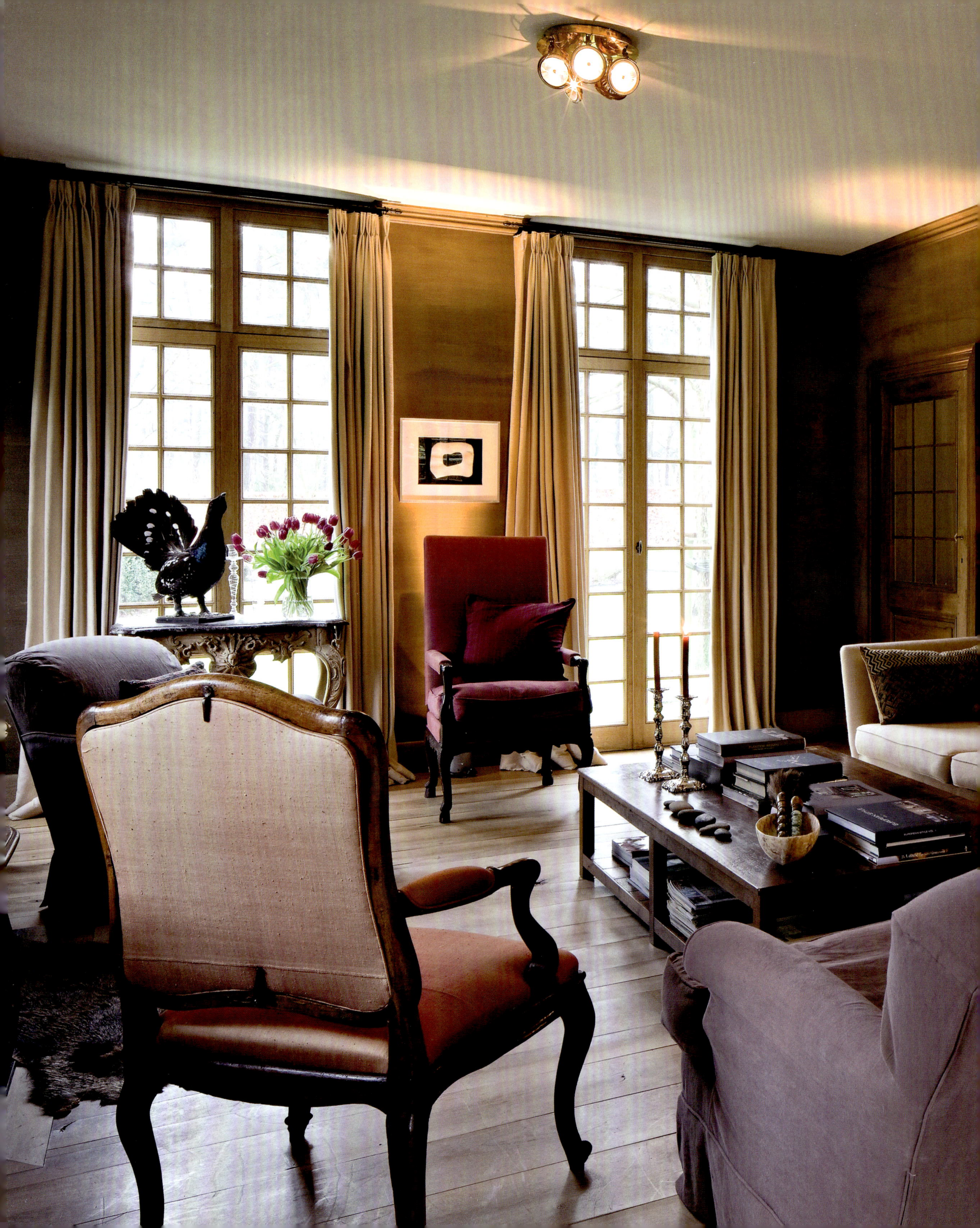

123

NEWLY BUILT AND STILL AUTHENTIC

This beautiful country mansion with unique panoramic views is situated in the middle of meadows in the Noorderkempen near Antwerp: an exceptional project by Porte Bonheur. By using old building materials and with an eye for detail, this house full of character has grown into a pleasant, attractive home, where sight has not been lost of modern-day living comfort.

www.portebonheur.be

Sand-coloured whitewashed walls.

↖
Whitewashed walls in
warm tints were chosen
everywhere.
The lamp hoods in linen
were made to measure.
An old terracotta floor (red/
black mixture).

TIMELESS MINIMALISM
IN A TRADITIONAL FARMHOUSE

Am projects, Mark Mertens got the commission to design and complete the interior of this farmhouse in West Flanders. Am projects were also in the running for the interior décor. The aim was a timeless, minimalist interior, which still radiated a certain warmth. Much use was made of natural materials throughout this project. Colour accents were added by the furniture and paintwork.

www.amprojects.be

The panelling around the fireplace was made of solid oak by Am projects. The doors are fitted with snap-locks. Furniture from the Am projects collection covered with Belgian and Italian linen. An antique Louis XIII bergère in walnut.

↖
The dining area was fully panelled and painted in an aubergine tint.
A hidden door with access to the bureau was made in the panelling.

AN INTERIOR WITH A SOUL

An interior with a soul: that was the wish of the residents. From this basis the interior architect from Vlassak-Verhulst carefully selected century's old recuperated materials and worked closely together with craftsmen who ensured a perfect integration of these historic elements in the home with contemporary home comfort. The finishing touch was created by the subtle use of old painting techniques and the furnishing by the antiquarian Garnier.

www.vlassakverhulst.be

View from the living area.

The dining room was painted in a homemade lime-wash. The furniture was provided by the antiquarian Garnier.

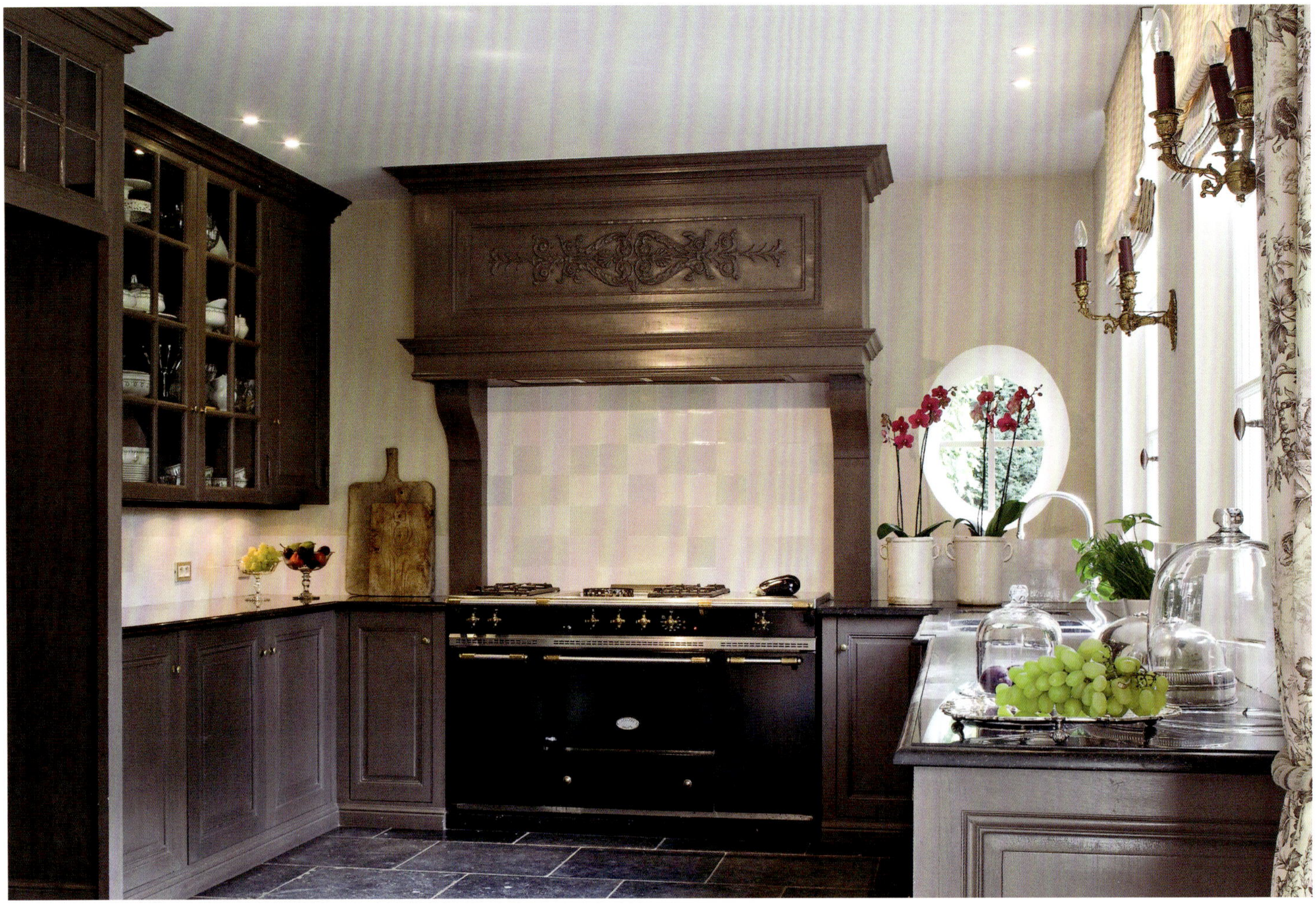

Ceiling high cupboards according to an old model, with hand applied patina.

Rouge belge and white Carrara marble in a classical floor pattern.

A LOVE OF ART, ANTIQUES
AND TRADITIONAL CRAFTS

The residents of this exceptional home on the Waal in Ridderkerk have a love of art and antiques and a true admiration for any authentic and handmade crafts. The interior design fits seamlessly to the philosophy of carefully selected recuperation materials, traditional woodwork and exceptional metal fittings. To allow some art objects to come into their own even more the decision was consciously made for intense colours and special painting techniques.

www.vlassakverhulst.be

Old terracotta tiles for the floor of this lavender blue linen room.

A trompe-l'oeil in this Italian inspired bathroom.

↖
The imposing entrance hall with monumental staircase. The sculpted grapevines on the pilaster are a wink at the profession of the residents.

AN EXCEPTIONAL COUNTRY HOUSE FOR PASSIONATE ANTIQUARIANS

Antiques dealer Jean-Philippe Demeyer and his colleagues, residents of the house, found this exceptional monument a few kilometers outside Bruges. It was the ideal place for them to receive customers and friends, to present antique collections and to talk about the furnishing of their homes and offices. The walled in home dates from the 13th century and is an example of the Bruges stepped gable gothic. What started as a small medieval country house or hunting lodge had grown by 2010 into a complex of buildings from different periods, in various styles and always in different bricks.

www.rooigem.com

The Chinese drawing room with turquoise velvet chairs from the 1940's and a 1970 red lacquered table and English arts and crafts, a Chinese inspired hanging light. A white woolen long-haired 1970 carpet and Napoleon III papier maché. A China club standing light. The walls are painted terracotta and then polished.

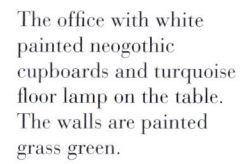

The office with white painted neogothic cupboards and turquoise floor lamp on the table. The walls are painted grass green.

The bathroom is bright blue with the central bath in front of the old mantelpiece.

↖
The library with an exceptional coloured Chinese carpet (c. 1940) and English easy chairs in harmony with the colours of the carpet.
The walls are painted in the same duck-egg green and then polished.

135

A DISTINCTIVE NEW VILLA IN WOODED SURROUNDINGS

This exclusive villa, situated in wooded surroundings, was recently constructed by the respected building contractor Belim Bouwteam to a design by architect Dirk Van Vlierberghe. The idyllic setting represented a particular challenge: to build a house that would suit the location. Partly thanks to the good relationship with the owners and the significant creative contribution made by the lady of the house, the result is a home that fits in perfectly with the owners' way of life.

www.belim.be

In the library and the sitting room, the aged-oak plank floor links the classic and the contemporary. The austere fireplace wall is softened by the use of shades of grey on the wall.

A wall separates the bedroom from the dressing room, which opens onto the corridor.

A SOPHISTICATED SENSE OF COLOUR

Gert Voorjans designed the interior of this house in the Waasland countryside: an eclectic look, with surprising colour choices and a fascinating mix of contemporary and antique elements.

www.gertvoorjans.com

Above the dining table is a 19th-century Moorish-style chandelier.
The walls of the dining room are presented as blocks, painted using two colours of casein paint. On the green wall is Martin Scholten's "Strumming Painter". In the foreground is a 19th-century industrial object.

↖
The classic cream-coloured hall was repainted in a typical Regency colour (Windsor green) to give more character to the central room of the house. The diptych above the door to the study is based on a painting by Veronese. A pair of vases from St-Paul de Vence, covered with colourful porcelain and ceramic pieces.

LIVING AMONGST COLOURS:
THE AUTHENTICITY OF LIME PAINTS

Arte Constructo has made a name for itself as an international distributor of natural, mineral and environmentally-friendly products and sound construction materials such as Unilit (natural hydraulic lime) and Coridecor (fine finishing products based on lime putty), and as an importer of Keim silicate paints. The Coridecor range consists of a variety of fine finishing products for different decorative purposes. Best results are achieved on mineral surfaces such as lime plaster, old layers of lime paint and porous stone or brick. The range offers a great deal of options, both for traditional and modern newly constructed interiors.

www.arteconstructo.be

Lime paints give distinctive buildings a unique look. Created by Bert de Waal.

Hand-coloured lime paints were selected for this house in the country. Created by Dankers Decor.

STREAMLINED, CLASSIC AND CHIC

Chris van Eldik and Wendy Jansen opened an interior-design company about ten years ago in Wijk bij Duurstede in the Netherlands, called De Zon van Duurstede (The Sun of Duurstede). Their style can best be described as "streamlined classic": a combination of warm, natural, honest, basic materials and fabrics, but in a definitely contemporary, almost minimalist setting. This husband-and-wife team were among the pioneers of lime paints, which have enjoyed great success in recent years. The choice of these paints is completely in keeping with their designs, which are timeless, sober and cosy, all at the same time.

www.zonvanduurstede.nl   www.jobinterieur.nl

Some examples from the Job collection: a corner unit in dark-grey linen, a Job 10 sofa bench with a low, studded rubber back and a Cristi XL sofa (bottom photo).

A Job 06 dining chair in pale linen beside an old oak table. Job 10 sofa bench without armrests, with a linen bathrobe by Society.

↖
The walls in this authentic fourteenth-century fireplace are in dark-grey lime paint. The original wooden floor has been given a dark-grey finish. Stijn sofa in a grey-green linen and a Hugo armchair in a brown fabric. A deep-pile carpet in wool and linen. The metal side tables were made specially for this project. On the left of the photo, an oak table with an X-frame. Curtains in a dark-brown, waxed fabric.

143

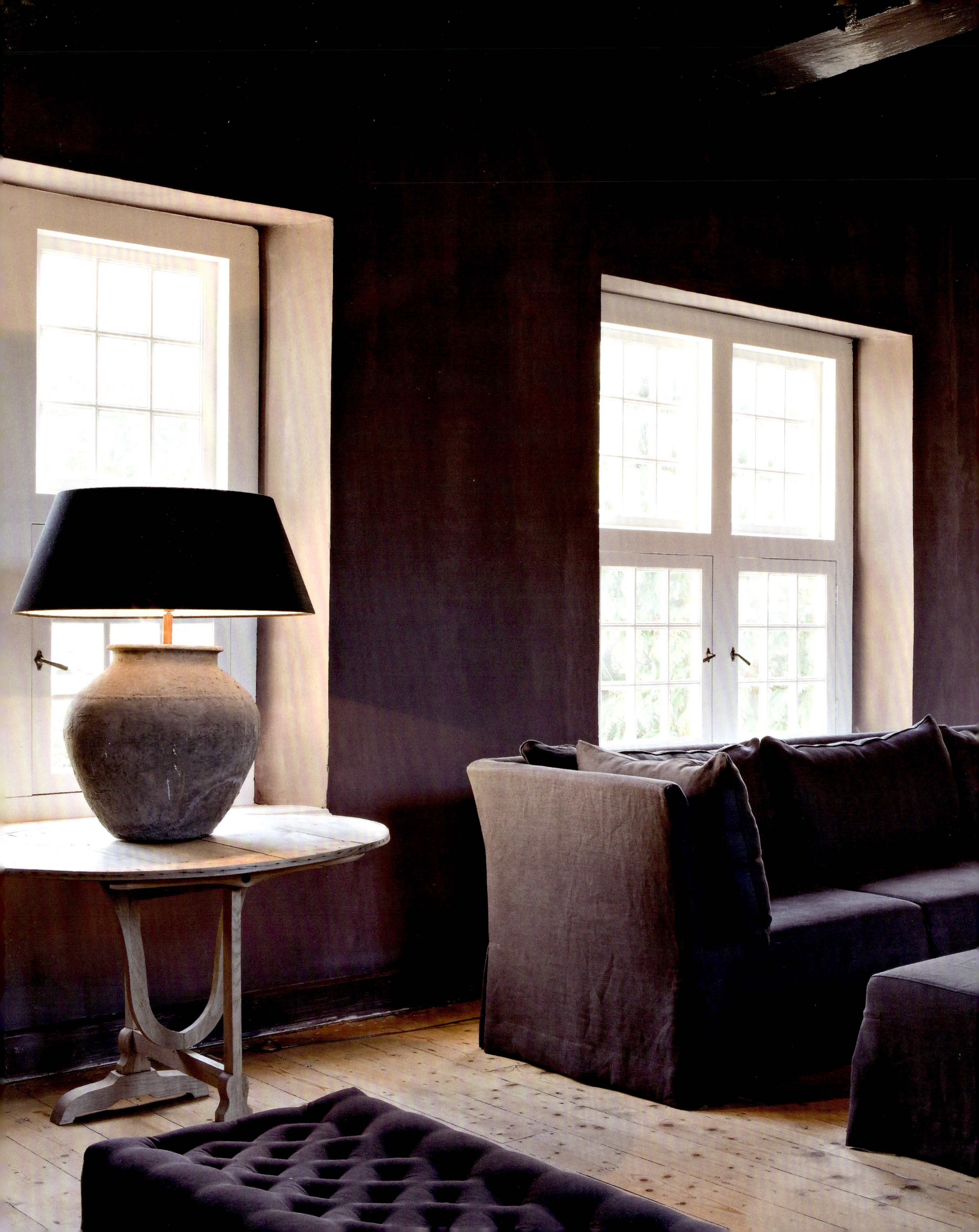

The corner unit consists of different elements with removable covers, in a dark-grey linen. In the background, a tall, narrow antique poplar-wood cupboard from northern Italy with its original grey-green patina. Left, an old wine table and an antique jar lamp with a black linen shade. Studded footstool.

The original backroom is now used as a sitting room, with built-in cupboard units. A Huygen sofa, two Stijn armchairs and a long coffee table in old wood. Chandelier by Van Brand and Van Egmond, in a black finish at the owners' request. Walls and cupboards in grey lime paint.

The comfortable sofa is upholstered in a purple linen fabric. Curtains in thick, pale linen lined with dark-grey acetate. Walls in brown lime paint.

This upstairs room has an oak floor. On the left-hand page, a Lodewijk armchair in linen. The open fireplace has been carefully restored. Walls in lime paint, Modular lighting.
Above and to the left, two sofa benches in silver rubber serve as desk chairs beside an antique painted double desk. In the foreground, a corner unit in a black linen fabric.

A RECENTLY BUILT COUNTRY HOUSE
WITH AN AGE-OLD PATINA

Although the country house in this report was constructed only recently, it seems to have a patina of great age. This is not only the result of the consistent use of weathered and reclaimed materials on the exterior, the interior also has a timeless, historic atmosphere. Dankers Decor, who have a royal warrant and are one of the most renowned Belgian decorating companies, created a harmony of colours throughout the whole house, using Arte Constructo's lime paints, coloured with natural pigments: an "à la carte" solution for this beautiful house.

www.arteconstructo.be   www.dankers.be

Many of the antique pieces of furniture have been collected by the family over the generations.

Here, Dankers Decor combined lime casein with green oxide. Curtains in fine silk, embroidered in Italy.

↖
The orange colour of this room was achieved by mixing Arte Constructo mineral lime paints with ground iron oxide.

A TASTEFUL RENOVATION
OF A HISTORIC NOTARY'S HOUSE

This notary's house dates from 1807. The exterior and interior of the building are both listed. The main building has all the charm of a grand, historic home. The extensions, designed by Stéphane Boens, have a more country feel and are completely integrated into their surroundings. Authenticity and simplicity were the most important principles in this project. White was therefore an obvious choice as the basic colour, as it emphasises the pure and beautiful character of the space.

www.brickinthewall.eu   www.stephaneboens.be

Frank Verschuere painted the walls in this listed, nineteenth-century notary's house using his own preparation of paint and clay.
Seating by Axel Vervoordt.

The dining room is in white lime paint. The chandelier dates from the late eighteenth century. A Spanish table in walnut wood, also from the eighteenth century (from am projects) and a pink cupboard that Frank Verschuere restored to its original condition. To the left of the pink cupboard, drawings by children. The oak parquet floor has been aged.

↖
The scullery is in old oak panels, painted with a traditional technique on the basis of clay and powder residue from a copper mine. The original bluestone steps lead to the dining room.

LIVING AND WORKING IN PERFECT HARMONY

Architect Lie Ulenaers faced an important challenge when designing her own home and work space. She had to combine a very compact private residence with an office on the first floor. The total design, furnishing and detailing result in an optimal division of both zones, which are still perfectly in harmony in a timeless atmosphere. The consistently thorough white/black highlights reinforce the spatial effect. White gives continuous nuances according to the incidence of the light. As a neutral background this colour also constantly contrasts with the people and objects in the interior. The limited materials and choice of colours ensure calm and coherence in all living spaces. The home was constructed in perfect consultation by the company Vincent Bruggen.

www.architectulenaers.be   www.vincentbruggen.be

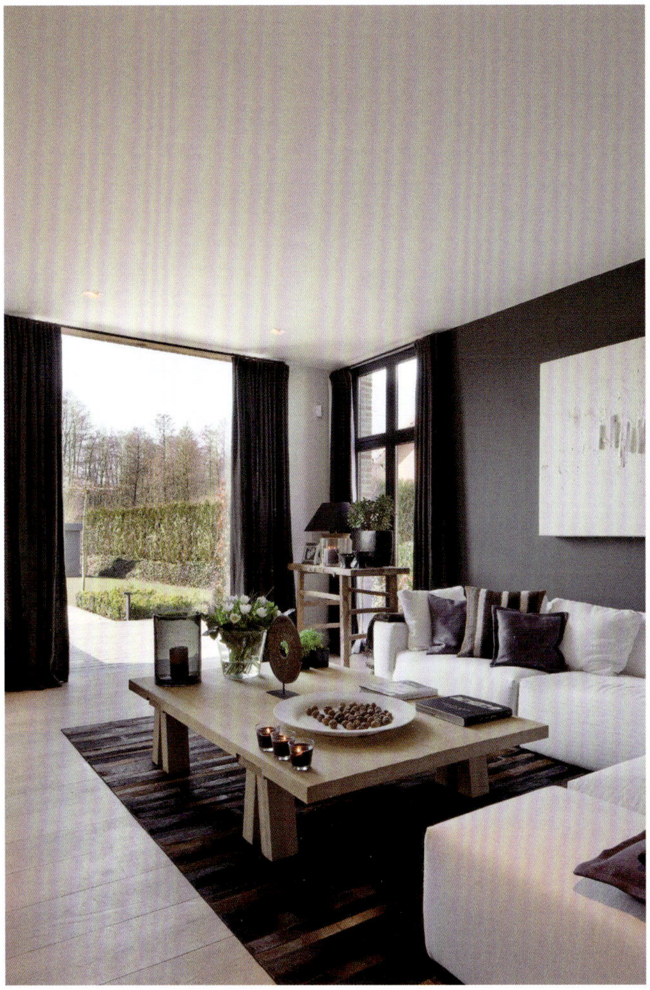
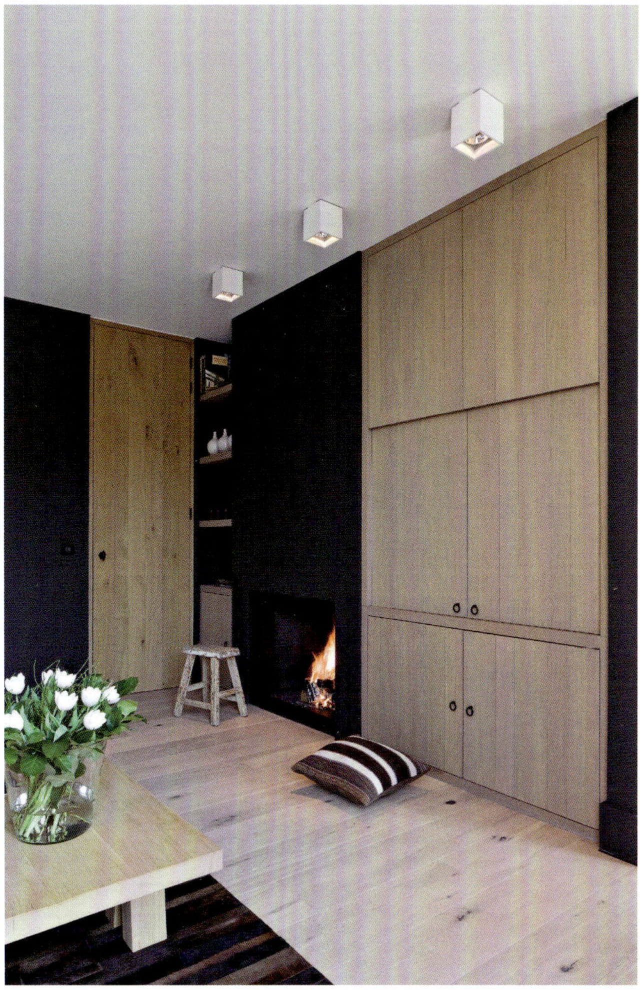

SOUL AND FEELING

This rehabilitation took place in a recently built house of 550 m². The new owner did not identify with the existing spaces and wanted to have a living space that fitted better with their image, so appealed to interior architect Guillaume Da Silva to give "soul and feeling" to this too conventional architecture.

www.guillaumedasilva.com

View from the kitchen to the living room: creation of perspectives and superposition of foregrounds and backgrounds. Posts structure and define the spaces while keeping them open.

The kitchen plays an important role.
The island realised in black granite structures the room and gives it its axes that define the preparation area and the dining area.
The cupboards make it possible to conceal all the technical elements.

↖
The living room axis is provided by the stained brushed and grooved oak chimneybreast.
Low table and lamps from Baxter. Sofa from Ascension Latore.

A UNIQUE BLEND

This apartment has been decorated by interior designer Axel Pairon:
a unique blend of warm and very colourful materials.

www.axelpairon.be

157

COSY LIVING

In close dialogue with interior designer Fabienne Dupont, the resident of this house wished to create a modern classic and cosy living atmosphere. She brought the dining table and chairs from her last home, and combined them with chairs by Philippe Starck and a Bomat carpet. The billiard room was painted dark purple by Fabienne Dupont; the billiard cloth was also renewed in the same colour.

www.alexandershouses.com   www.fabathome.be

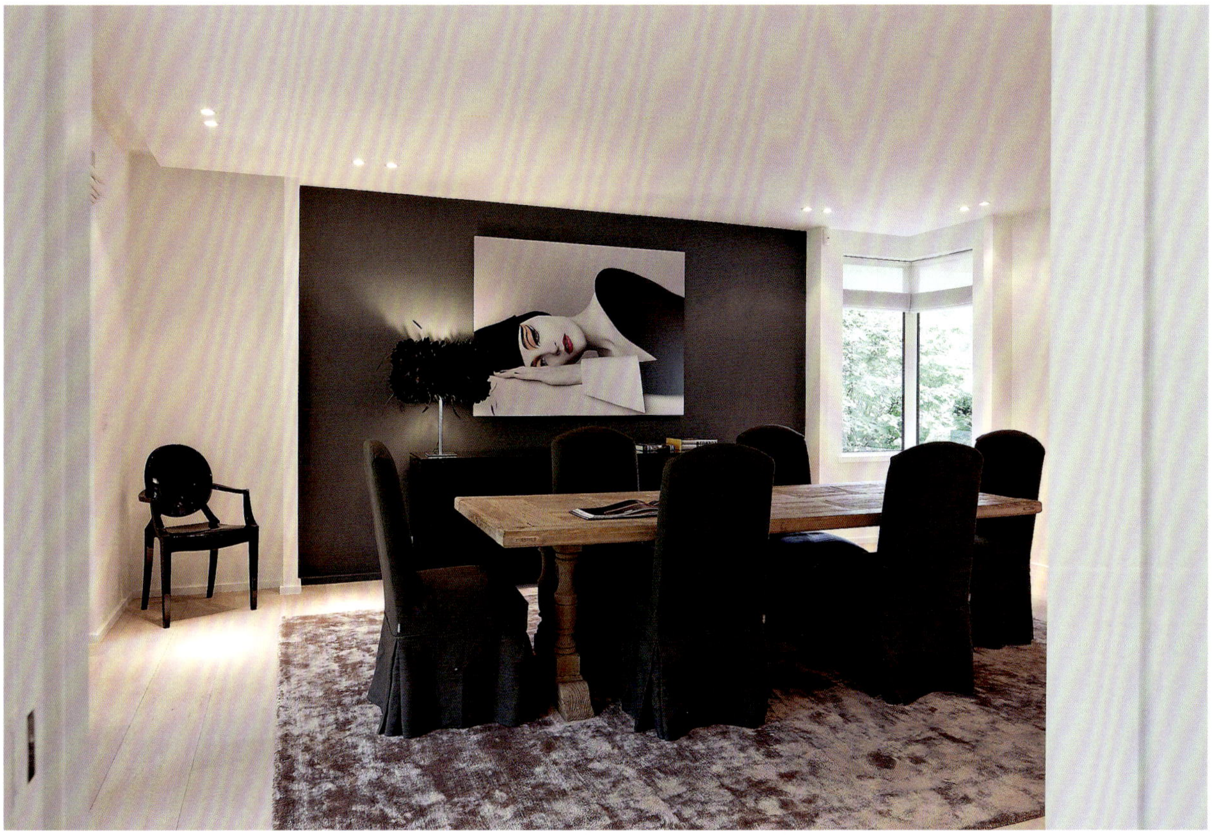

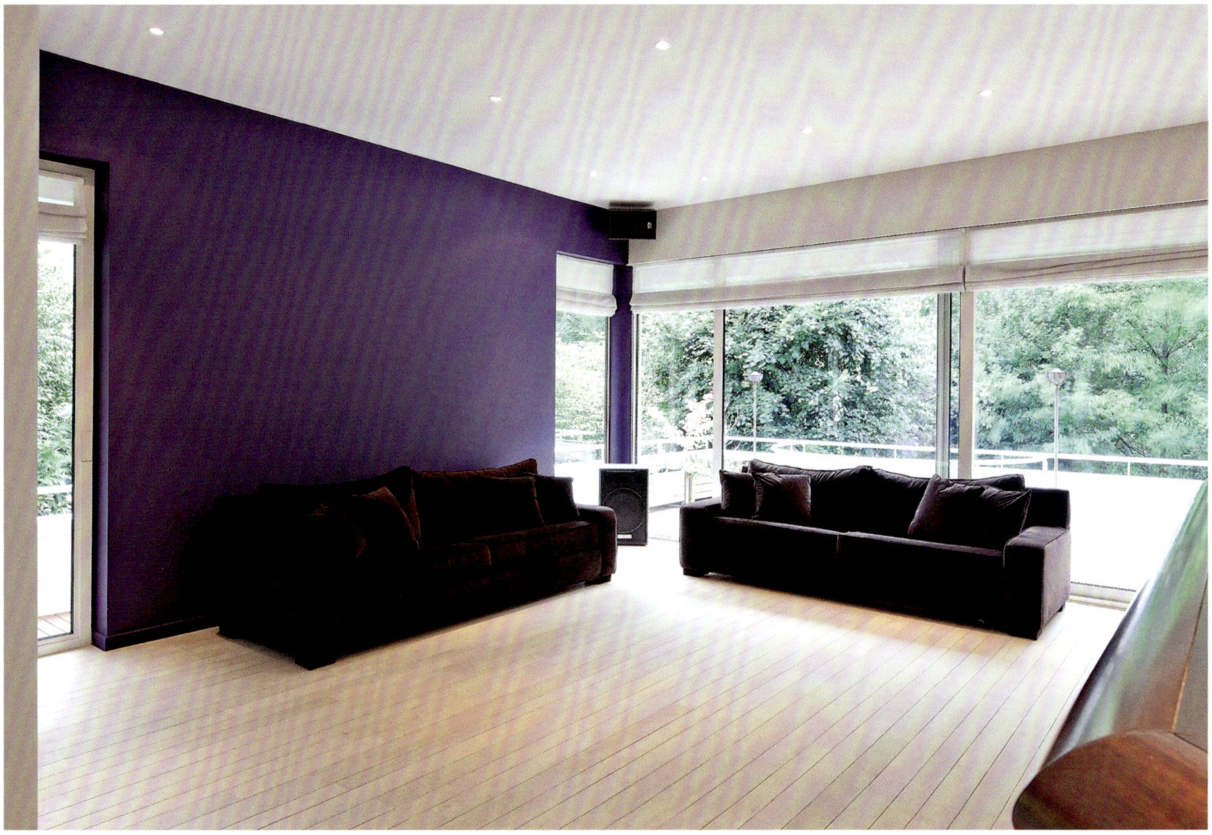

THE BEAUTY OF LIME PAINTS

In this project, Chris van Eldik and Wendy Jansen have used lime paints to create a unique and timeless atmosphere.

www.zonvanduurstede.nl   www.jobinterieur.nl

161

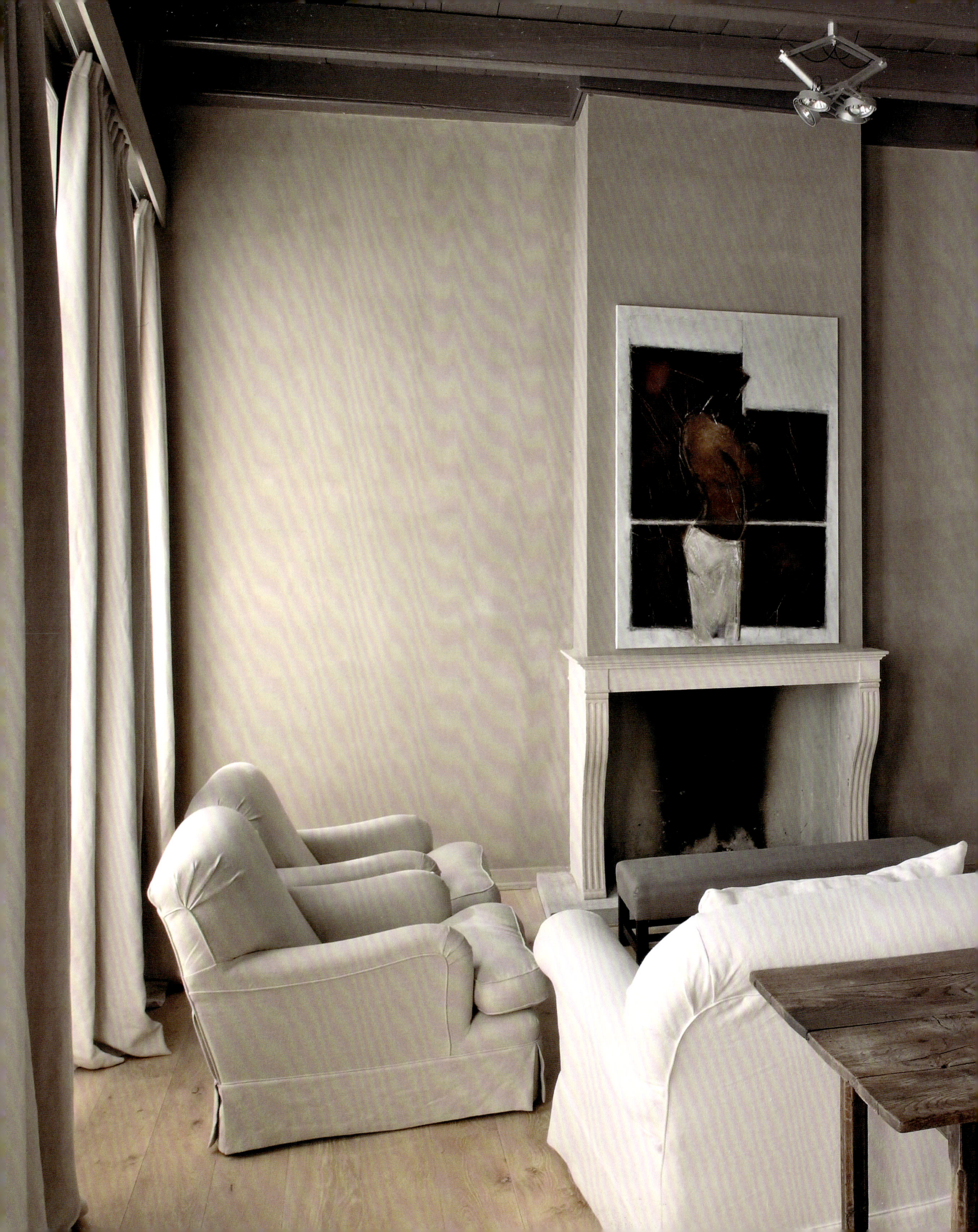

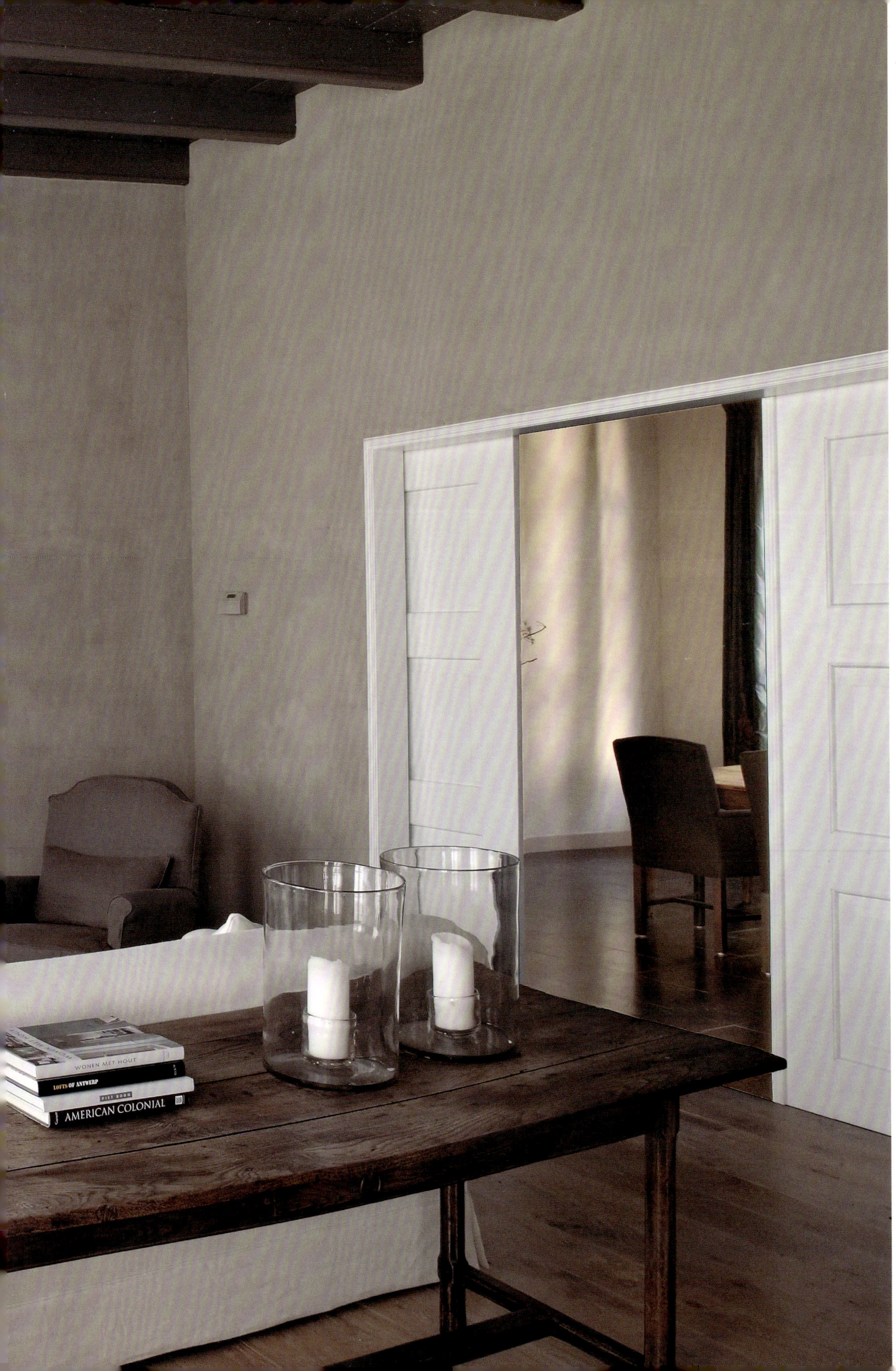
WONEN MET HOUT
LOFTS OF ANTWERP
AMERICAN COLONIAL

A CLASSIC VILLA WITH CONTEMPORARY DETAILS

Costermans Villa Projects has built this classic French manor style villa in the green outskirts of Antwerp.

www.costermans-projecten.be

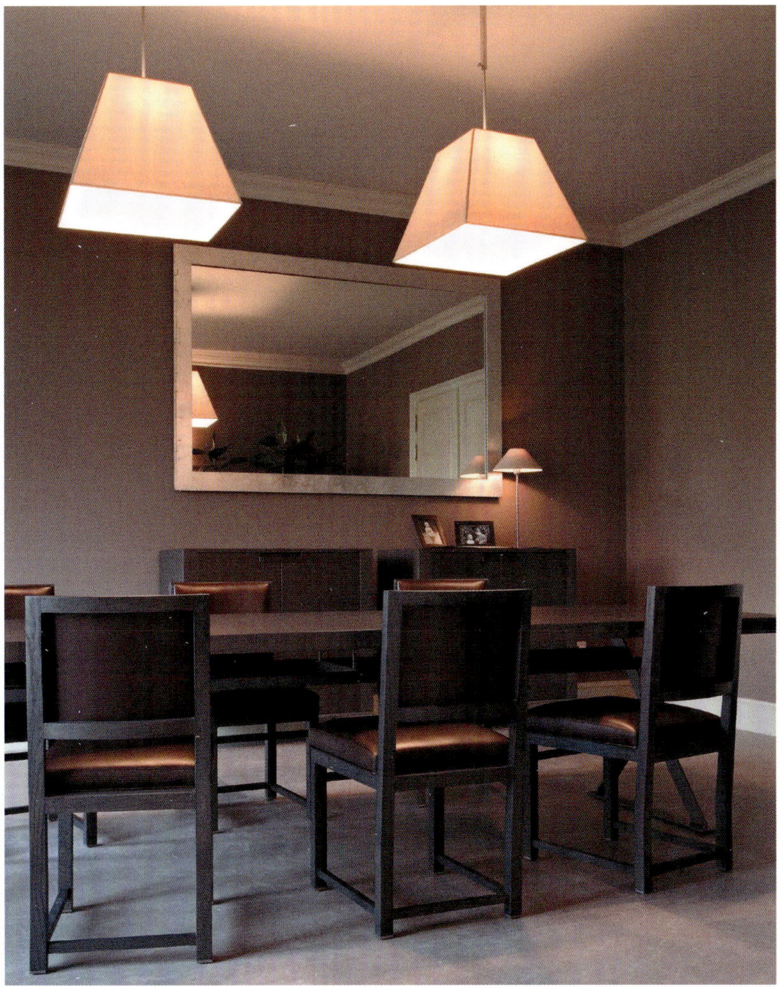

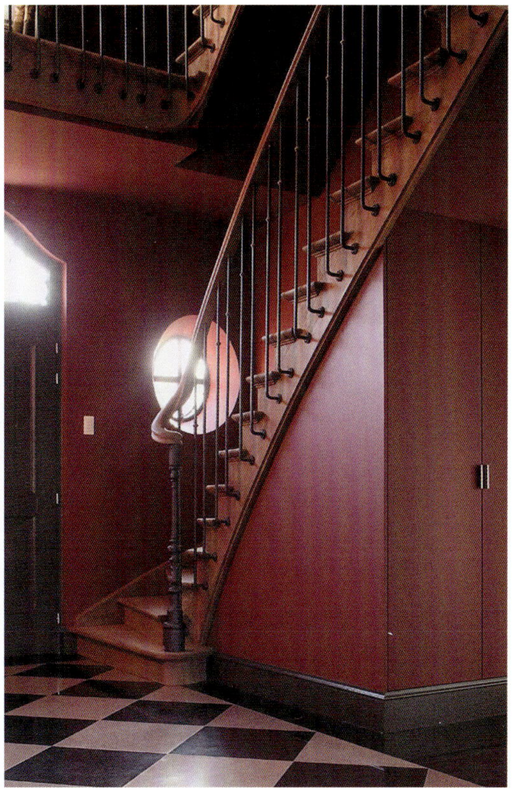

FAMILY LIFE

They wanted light parquet but fell for a shiny black floor. And they loved it. No other solution seemed to bring such harmony to the overall project. Unconditional supporters of the Lempereurs' work, the owners trusted them from beginning to end. They also followed their advice for the design of an area entirely dedicated to their three children, in order to keep another one reserved for the parents. They agreed to the wonderful idea of designing the bathroom as an opening onto the Milky Way. The walls are covered with mosaic between amethyst and sky blue which allows a few stars to shine through. The lighting augments the scintillating aspect of the room. The furniture and the closets were made to measure, neatly dressing up even the smallest spaces.

www.olivierlempereur.com

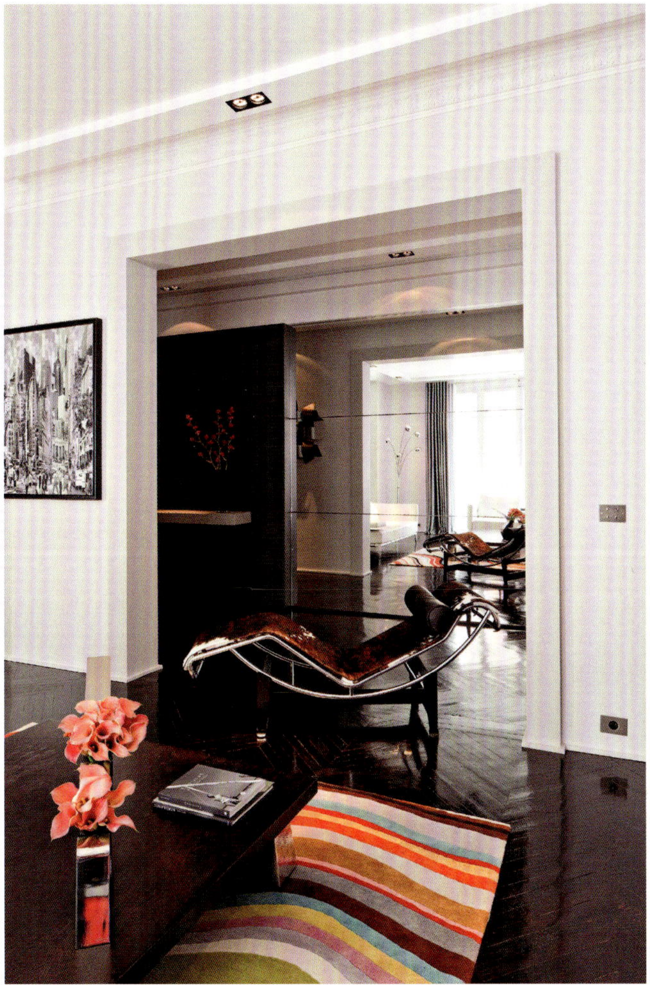

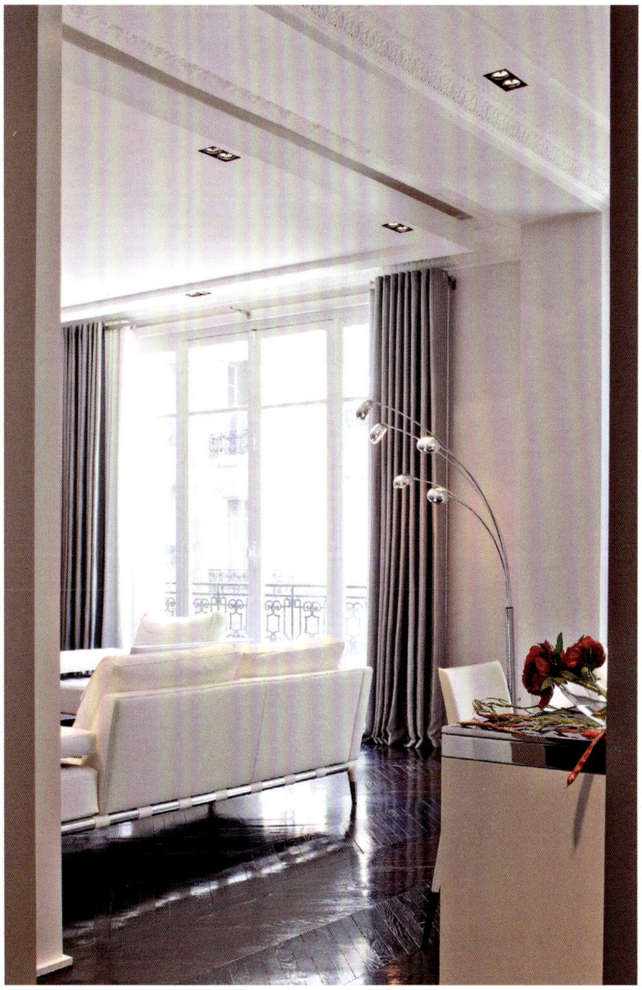

A DISCRETE METAMORPHOSIS

A rustic villa was transformed into a great comfortable and pleasant contemporary living environment. The traditional character was preserved but was given a contemporary "look". The old fireplace was kept in the living room, the parquet floor with broad floorboards was bleached.

www.alexandershouses.com

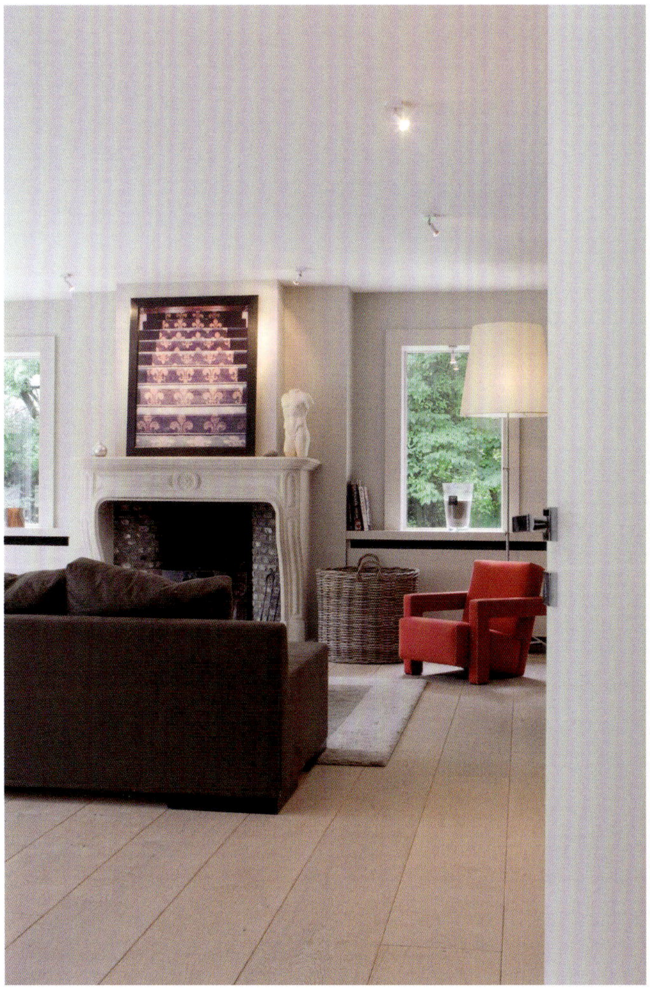

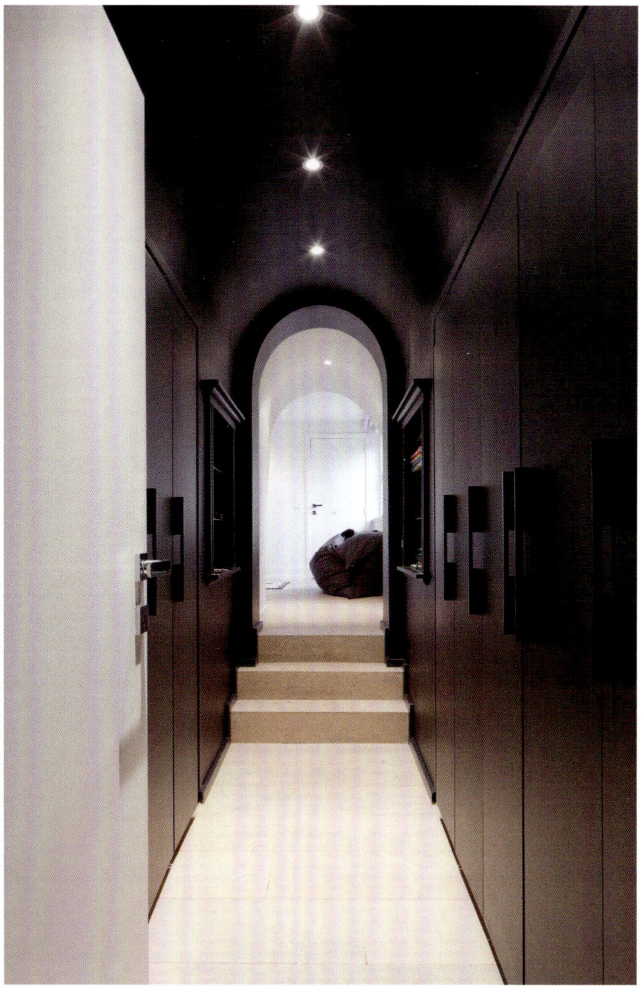

A SUCCESSFUL START

This was Alexander Cambron's first project: the beginning of a career full of exciting, exclusive homes. This existing, small villa was transformed into a living environment with a lot of space and a sea of light. The house was extended with a huge wooden orangery, the existing outside walls remained intact, with new window openings as a passage between the two living rooms. The living space is a single large whole, with living room, dining room and kitchen. The renovation was realised according to the style of the house, rustic and yet with a modern touch. It is a real family home where everyone has their place, from young to old.

www.alexandershouses.com

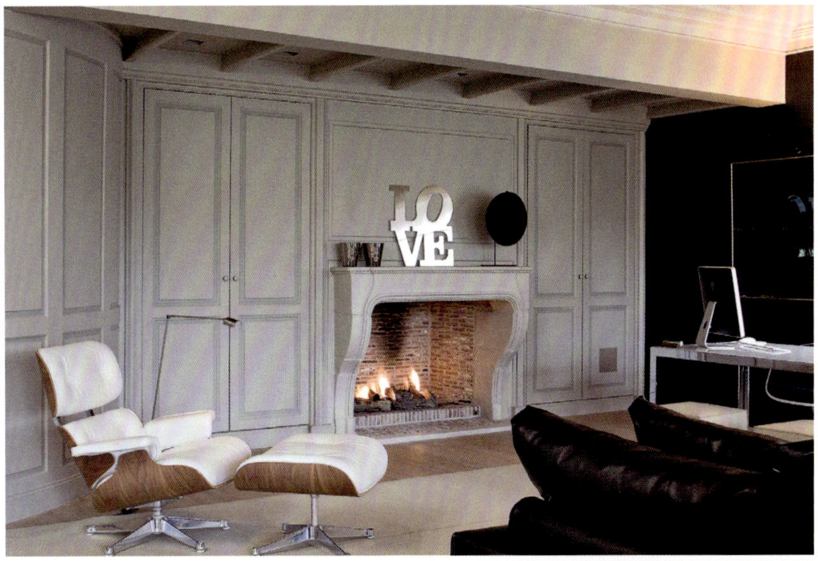
LO
VE

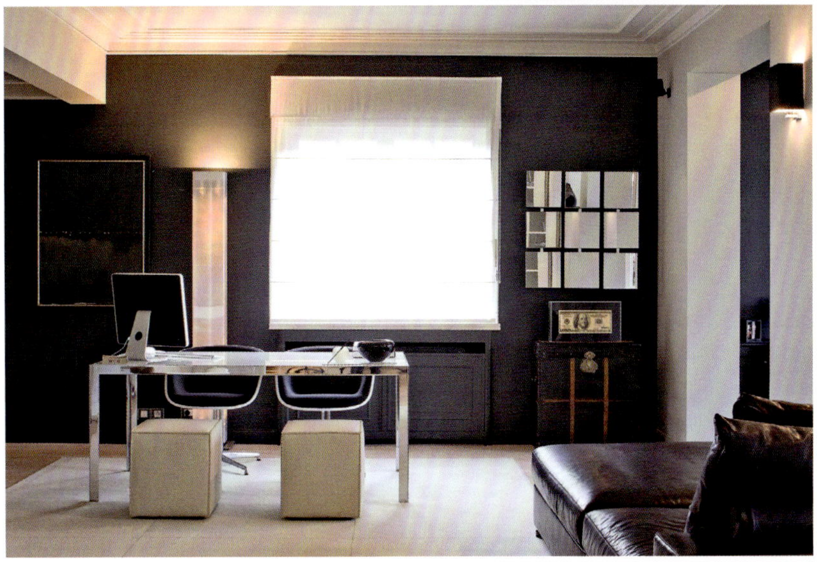

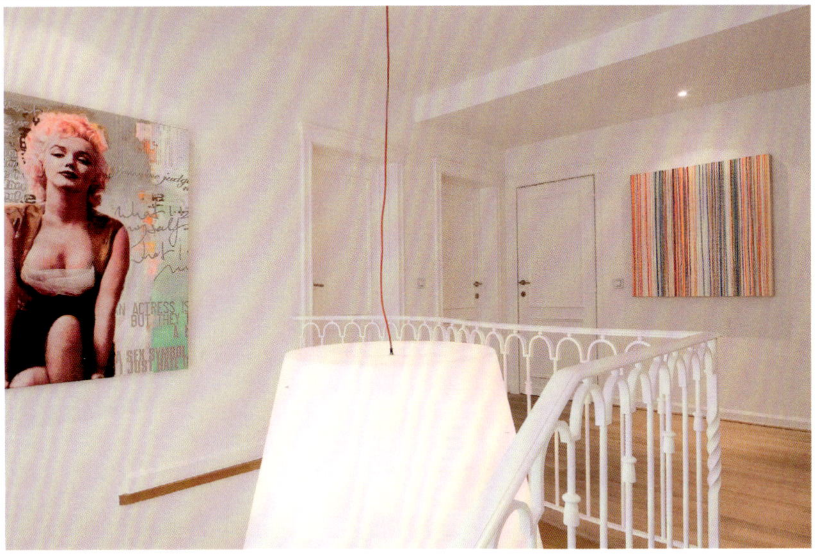

THE METAMORPHOSIS OF A FARMHOUSE INTO A COUNTRY MANOR HOUSE

Tradiplan, the exclusive home construction company, ensured the successful transformation of this modest farm with a small residential section and a number of stables into a charming country manor house with generous proportions. Only the exterior walls of the original farmhouse remain standing: all of the rooms inside have been redesigned and the stables have also been equipped as living areas. The owners, who work in the hotel sector and are passionate about interior design, have created a look that radiates both timeless class and simple rural charm.

www.tradiplan.be

Two old varieties of marble have been laid in a checked design: small tiles in the hall and larger ones in the dining room.

In the kitchen, old terracotta tiles have been combined with oak kitchen units that have been clad with natural stone. The wall tiles are antique Dutch 'witjes'.

↖
The owners have created a very personal interior with a number of valuable antique pieces of furniture. They also attach a great deal of importance to details: the switches were inspired by old models that were often used in farmhouses.

173

A PERFECT BALANCE
BETWEEN CLASSIC AND MODERN

Benedikte Lecot is an interior designer who aims to create a symbiosis of functionality, atmosphere, light and architecture in all of her projects. She aims to achieve a unity of style within a pleasant living environment that balances classic and modern, and which is always in keeping with the individual needs and desires of the client. All of her designs are therefore created à la carte. The exclusive character of her interiors is further reinforced by perfect workmanship, carried out by experienced and passionate professionals.

www.b-lecot.be

The extra-wide oven is integrated into a ceiling-height wall-unit. The cooking island stands in a central position.

A symbiosis of classic and contemporary in this office: a fitted carpet in a plain, warm shade and a classic armchair have been combined with an ultramodern artwork.

↖
Oiled-white solid-oak floor.
The high MDF skirting boards have been painted white.
Work of art with artichoke by Ria de Henau.

A FASCINATING MIX OF OLD AND NEW

Jan Smits and Kathy Alliët, managers of the interior design store Pas-Partoe, show in this project how old and new can be perfect partners. The new building serves as showroom, while the old rectory serves as the family home and at the same time alludes to the lifestyle philosophy of Pas-Partoe. The house shows a fascinating, surprising mix of ambience, proportions, shapes and materials amidst renowned collections (Promemoria, Flexform, Knoll, Maxalto) as well as the residents' own creations. The many different facets of living are perfectly matched here.

www.pas-partoe.be

In the centre, an Aga cooker with black Moroccan tiles above.
The horizontal wooden shutters were given an ebony colour.
The large, austere window, in a steel framework,
offers a beautiful view of the pond.

The ancient old sink from the original kitchen was
given a new lease of life in the cloakroom.
On the right a view of the pantry.

↖
Contrast between dark and
light, straight and curved
lines, and contemporary and
classical art.
The old cement tiles were
restored.

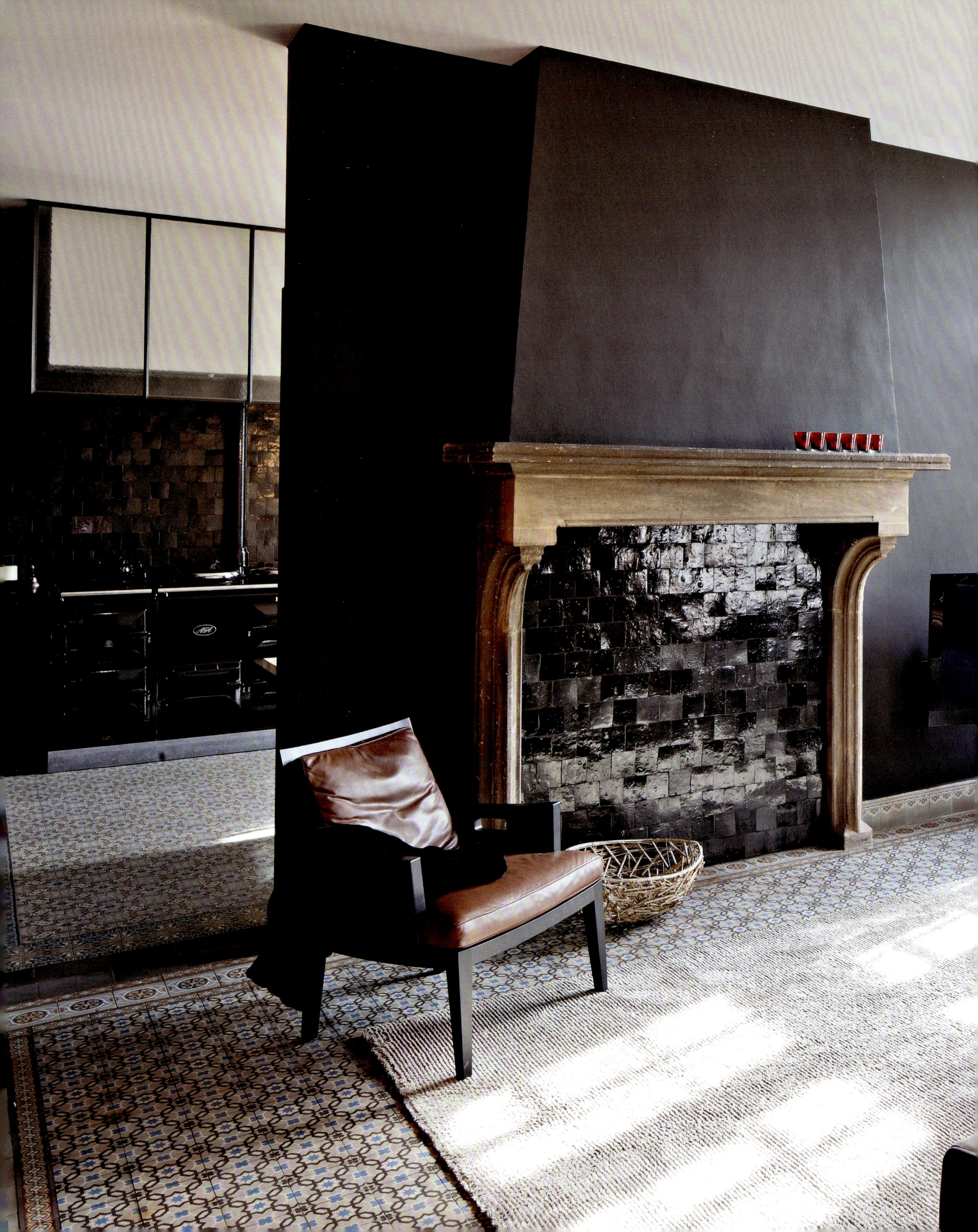

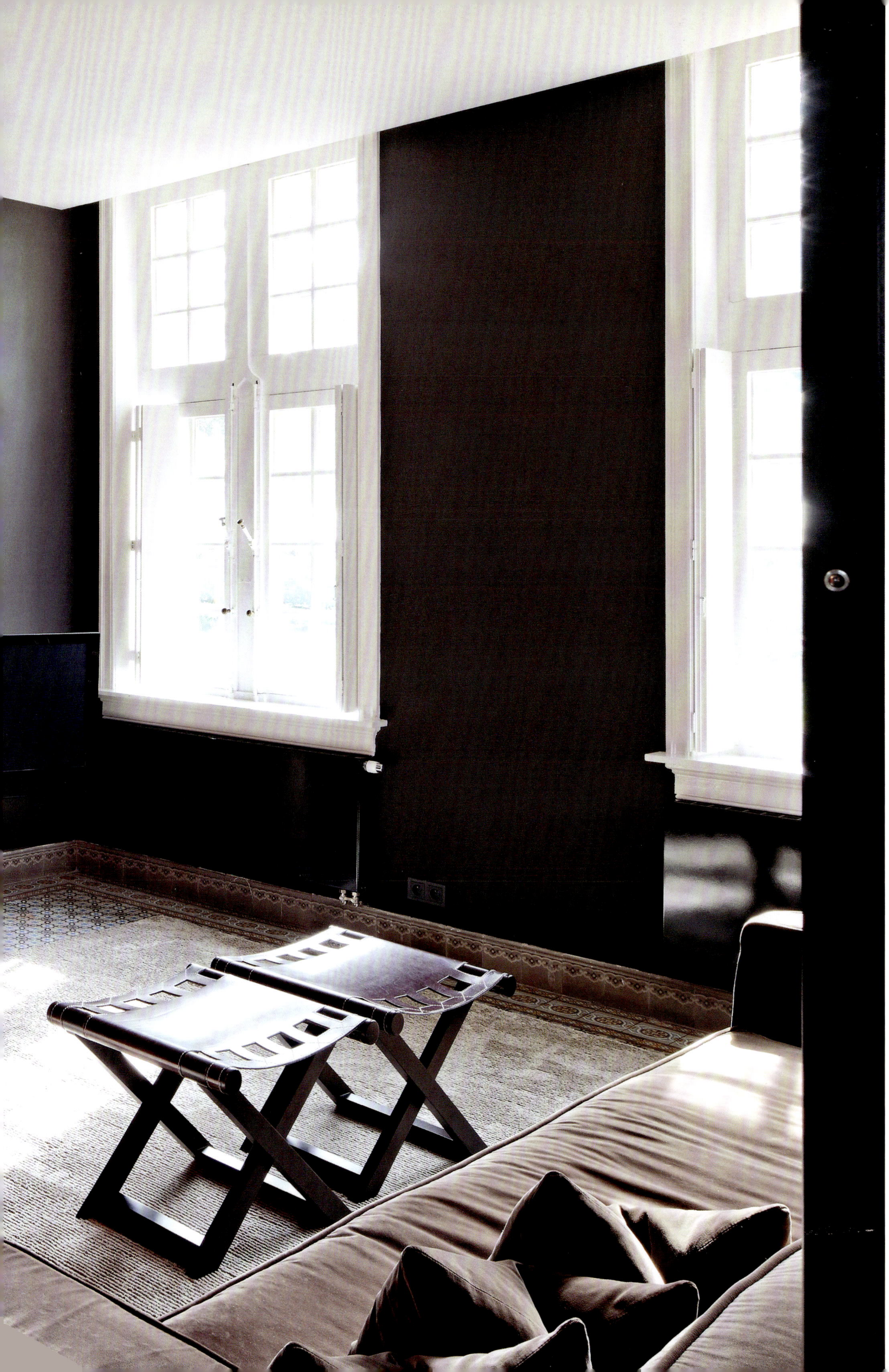

In the dining room, a solid wood table is combined with the Tulip chairs by E. Saarinen and a chandelier by Piet Boon. The artwork in plexiglass frame is by Guy Leclef. The big photograph is by Verne.

A mix of different seats in various materials for the lounge. The leather pouffe and the bronze side tables are on wheels.

The carpet is made from cowhides.

SPACE AND LIGHT
IN A CONTEMPORARY COUNTRY HOUSE

This stately mansion was designed in 2009 by architect Philippe Mortelmans at the behest of a family with three young children. The interior is a creation of Annick Grimmelprez. The house is idyllically situated in Schilde, a green suburb close to Antwerp. Each room offers a view of the protected forest area and this house is perfectly matched to the wishes of the owners: contemporary, with a strong feeling of light and space, where precious materials have been used and a few colourful highlights. The result: a cosy home in an oasis of tranquillity and wellness.

info@annickgrimmelprez.be

The entrance hall, refined to the strictly essential, provides direct access to the garden. The Pietra di Medici stone staircase forms a central theme in the different living levels. On the ground floor, the hall was decorated with an antique Chinese console table and a canvas by Miguel Ybanez. The guest toilet is finished with a silver-coloured stucco wall. A basin in Pietra di Medici.

↖
View from the entrance hall to the dining room. The oak flooring was installed throughout the house. All walls are in violet-coloured mineral paint, curtains in silver taffetas and velvet.
The wall light fittings have a satin nickel finish and there is an antique Chinese dining table and console tables. Leather upholstered dining chairs designed by Christian Liaigre.
Artwork in monochrome ceramic by Jeanne Opgenhaffen.

THE ATTRACTIONS OF AN ANCIENT FARMHOUSE

The Heerlijkheid van Marrem is a genuine farmhouse whose oldest remnants date from the seventeenth century. The «poorthuys» (gatehouse), the stable wing, the «graenschuur» (granary) and the walls have all been given heritage status by the Department of Monuments. The farm was in a terrible condition when the current owners bought it three years ago. In consultation with an enthusiastic builder and site supervisor, and without using an architect, they turned the semi-ruin into a charming home with all modern comforts. The house (the most recent wing of the property) was no more than a shell, so this meant that the new owners could do what they wanted.

www.heerlijkheidvanmarrem.be   www.amprojects.be   www.vandemoortel.be

The guest room with small bathroom. Marie Vandemoortel supplied all the reclaimed materials.

↖
All the antique furniture in the entrance hall was found at am projects.

A UNIQUE COUNTRY HOUSE IN FLEMISH STYLE

This unique Flemish country house is one of the finest works by Ramen Lanssens of Dentergem: tough, massive shed doors with the craftsman wrought fastenings from the forge of Dujardyn artconcept of Oostrozebeke. The classic Flemish painted cross windows, based on an 18th century design, with outer hatches, the various oak outside doors with stylish rod division ... everything was custom built in the workshops of Ramen Lanssens.

www.laramen.be   www.dujardyn.com

↖
The hand wrought cupboard handles, door handles and bell on the front door were made by Dujardyn artconcept.

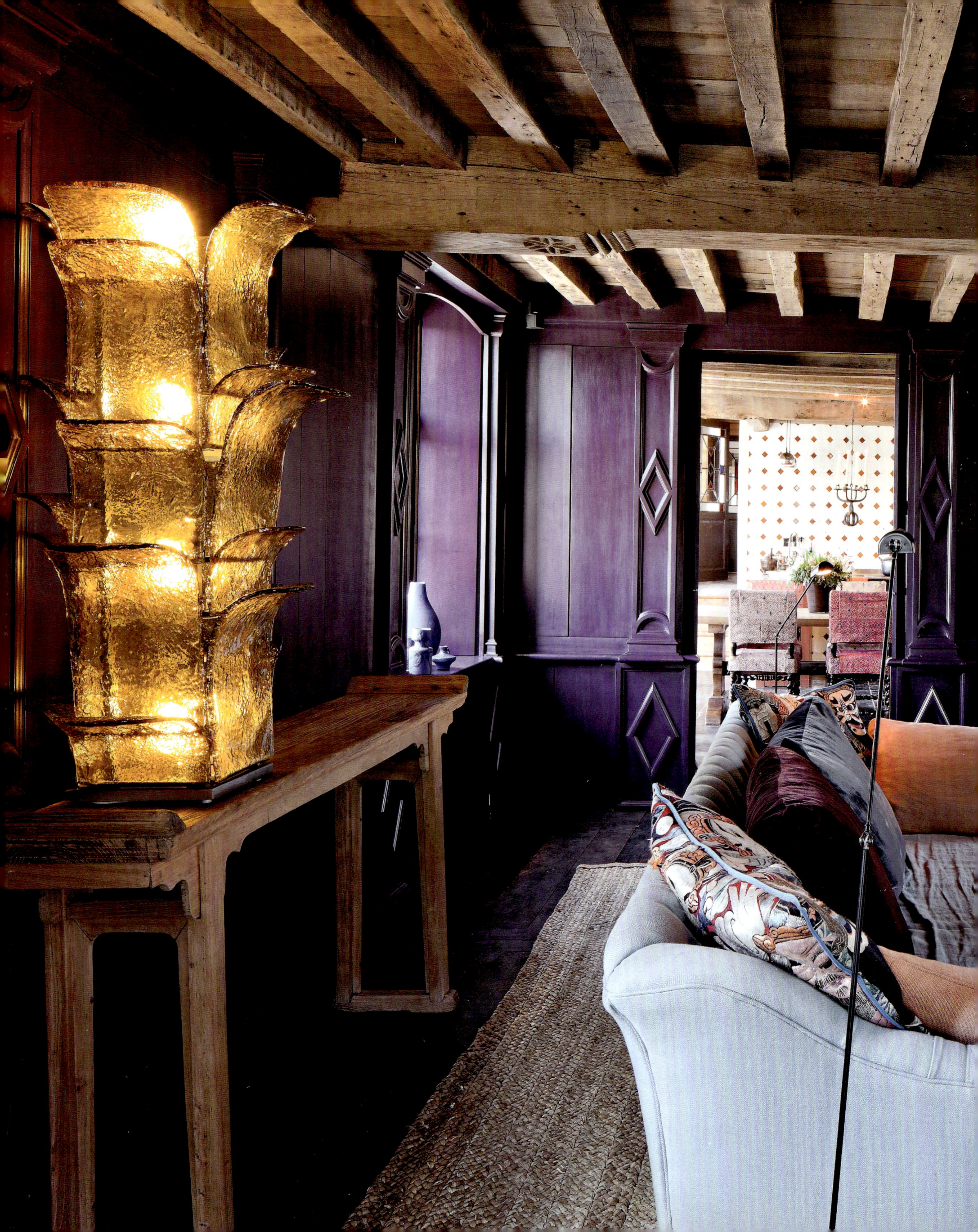

189

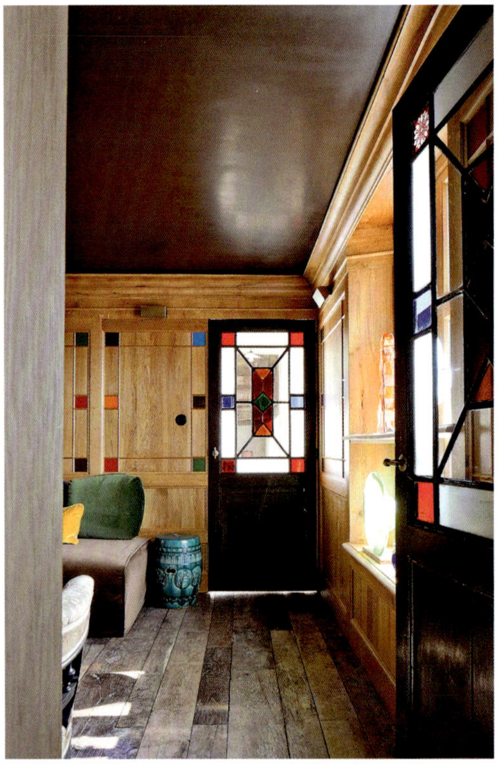

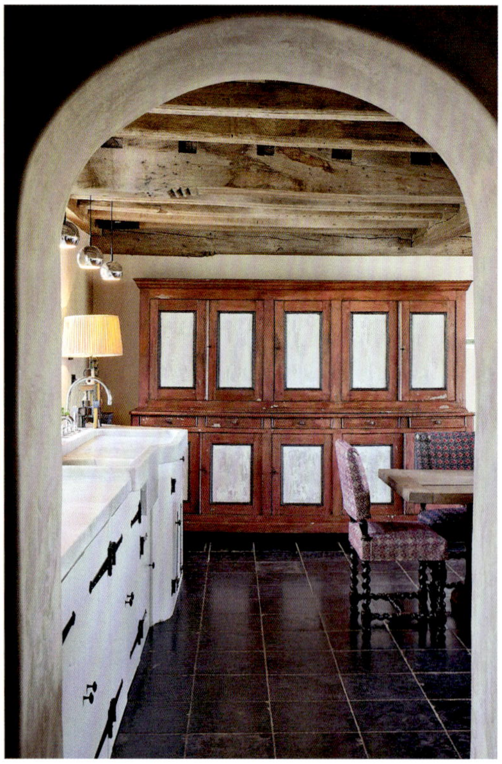

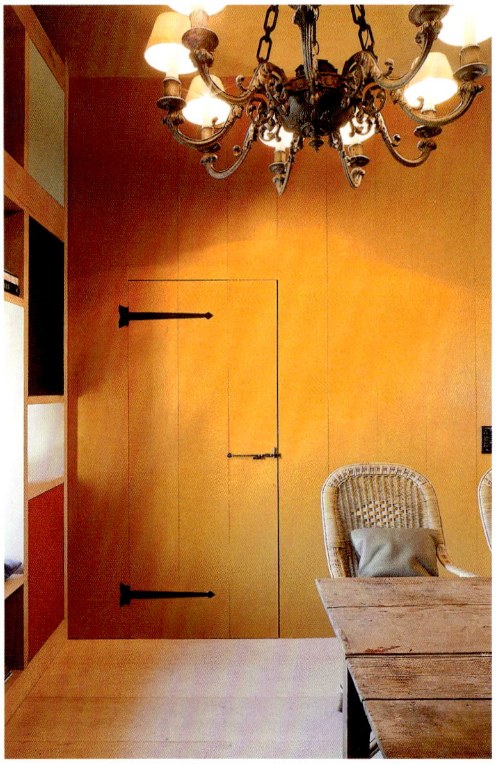

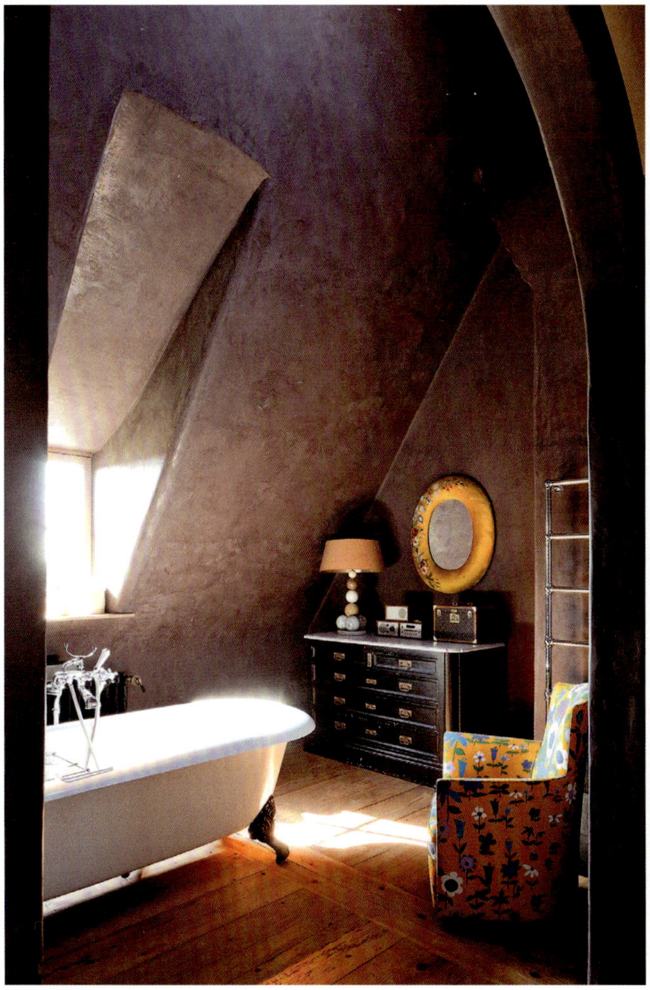

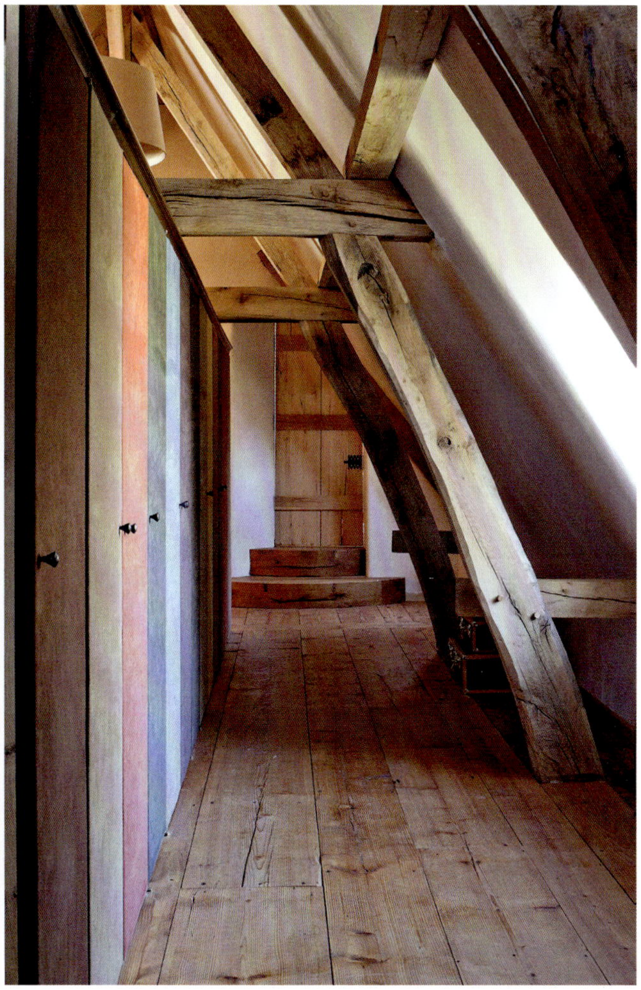

RESTORATION OF AN 18TH CENTURY BREWERY

Beer has been brewed in this brewer's house with adjacent outbuildings since 1730. Everything was restored in style and harmony by interior designer Virginie Vrydaghs, who left the original structure and decorations intact. The rusted metal work was restored or reforged in the same authentic manner in the workshops of Dujardyn artconcept. During the renovation of the interior design, Virginie Vrydaghs aspired to retain the original charm and atmosphere of the house. Warm bold colours and old objects form a cleverly interwoven whole: a contemporary touch with timeless appeal.

www.dujardyn.com   www.virginievrydaghs.com

Lighting made from an antique Han vase. Antiques and furniture from Virginie Vrydaghs.

The original checkerboard flooring and panelling with Delft tiles were also retained.

↖
The old wooden floor in the front room is authentic and was sanded. The large settee was upholstered in orange-red velvet by Virginie Vrydaghs. The red-white veined marble fireplace was already in the house. Here under the whitewashed walls they found the authentic, almost completely faded inscriptions of the so-called conscripts from the time of Napoleon.

The original painted ceiling was retained. The old flooring was hand scoured and brushed.

The old elm wood staircase was restored to its former glory and covered in knotted wool English carpet.

The bathroom floor was covered with an English wool herringbone carpet.
The bath surround and washbasin are clad with buxy cendré stone.

A PASSION FOR BEAUTY

In this project, the architect Stéphane Boens deals in a masterly way with the rich architectural heritage adding a very personal touch to it. In close consultation with the owners, Boens created a unique home where tradition and artisanal techniques, modern comfort and a passion for beauty merge into a uniquely harmonious whole.

www.stephaneboens.be   www.obumex.be

Katrien De Keersmaecker (Obumex) was responsible for this project at Obumex. In close dialogue with the owners, high quality furniture was chosen mainly from Promemoria and Liaigre.

In the foreground a pouffe by Christian Liaigre ("Galet") in leather and walnut. Behind stand two armchairs + an Aziza pouffe from Promemoria. A lamp from Liaigre in bronze with a shade in watercolour paper. The desk lamp is a creation by Promemoria in bronze, with a cotton shade.

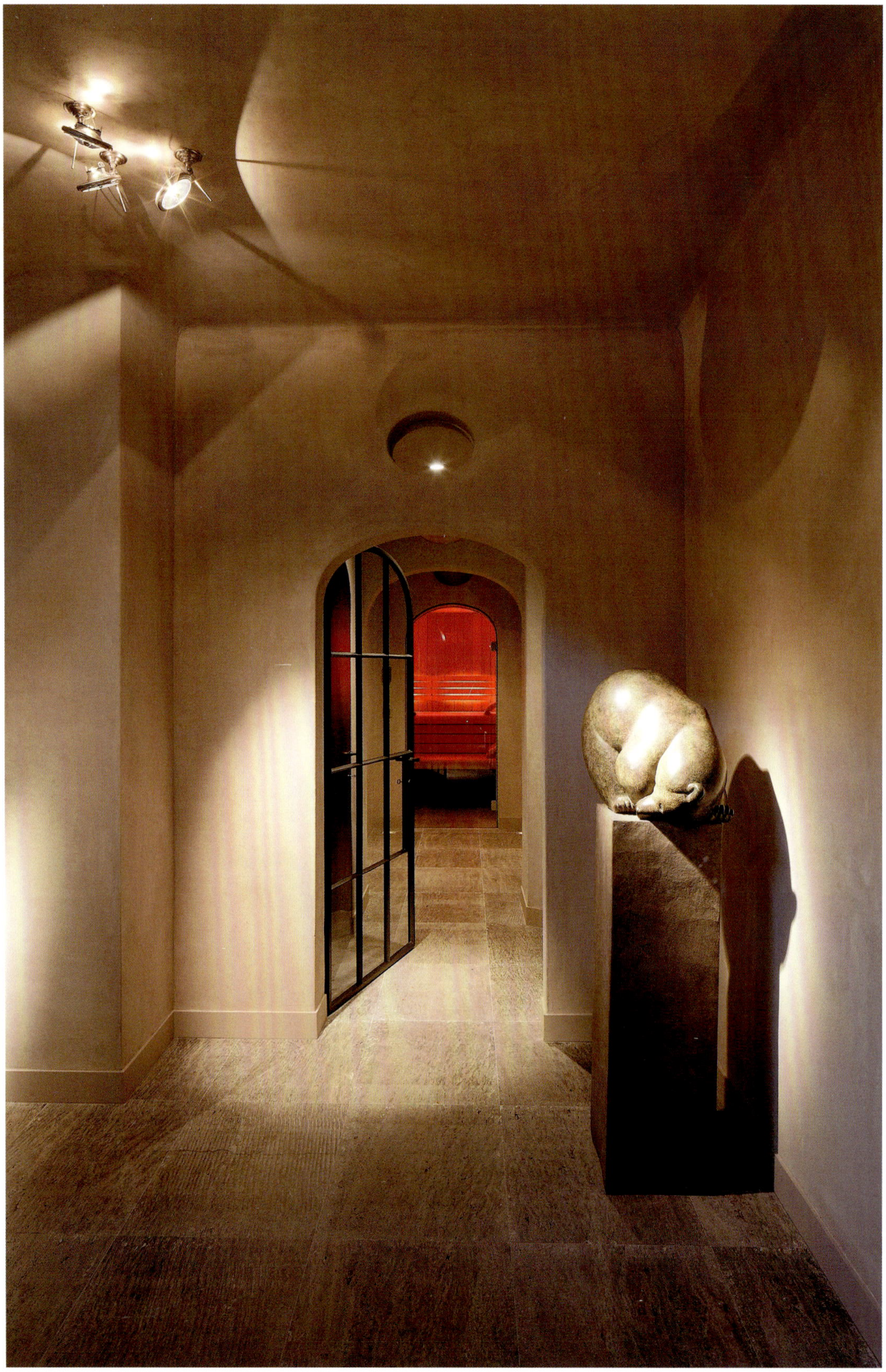

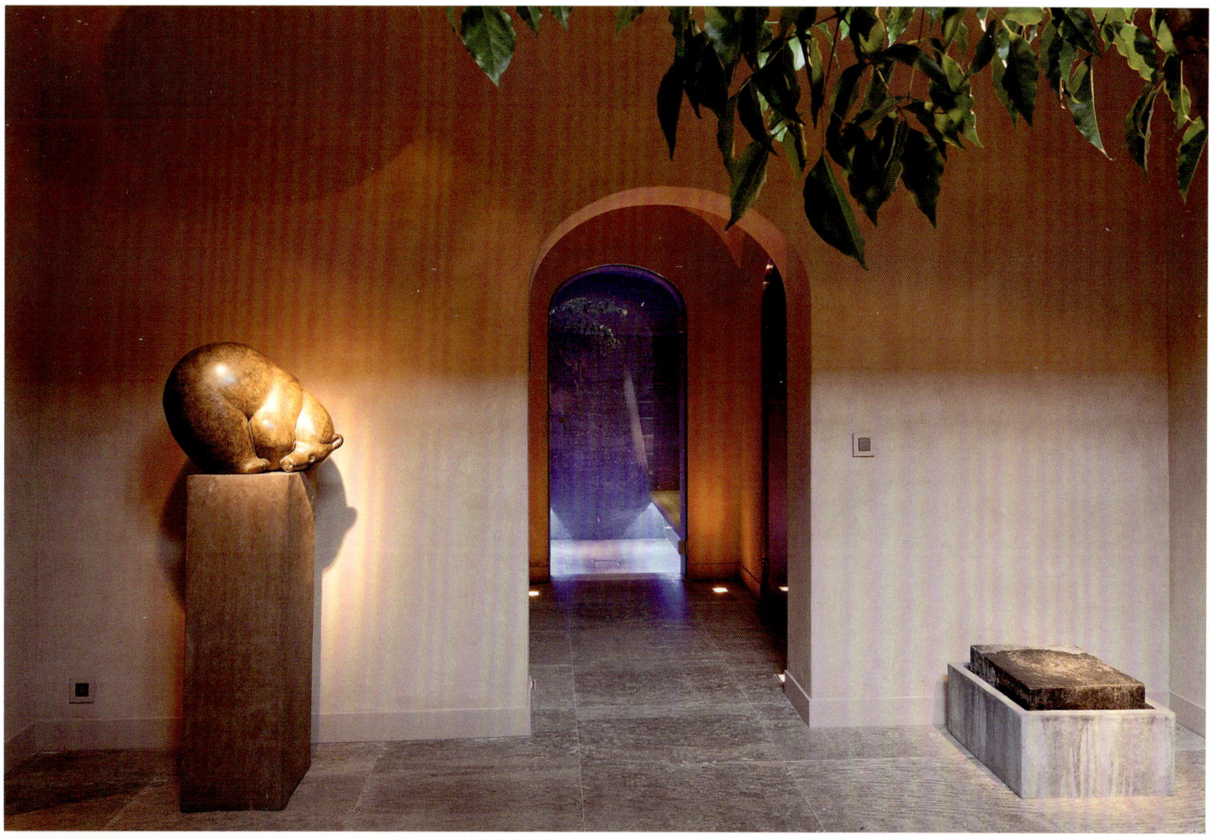

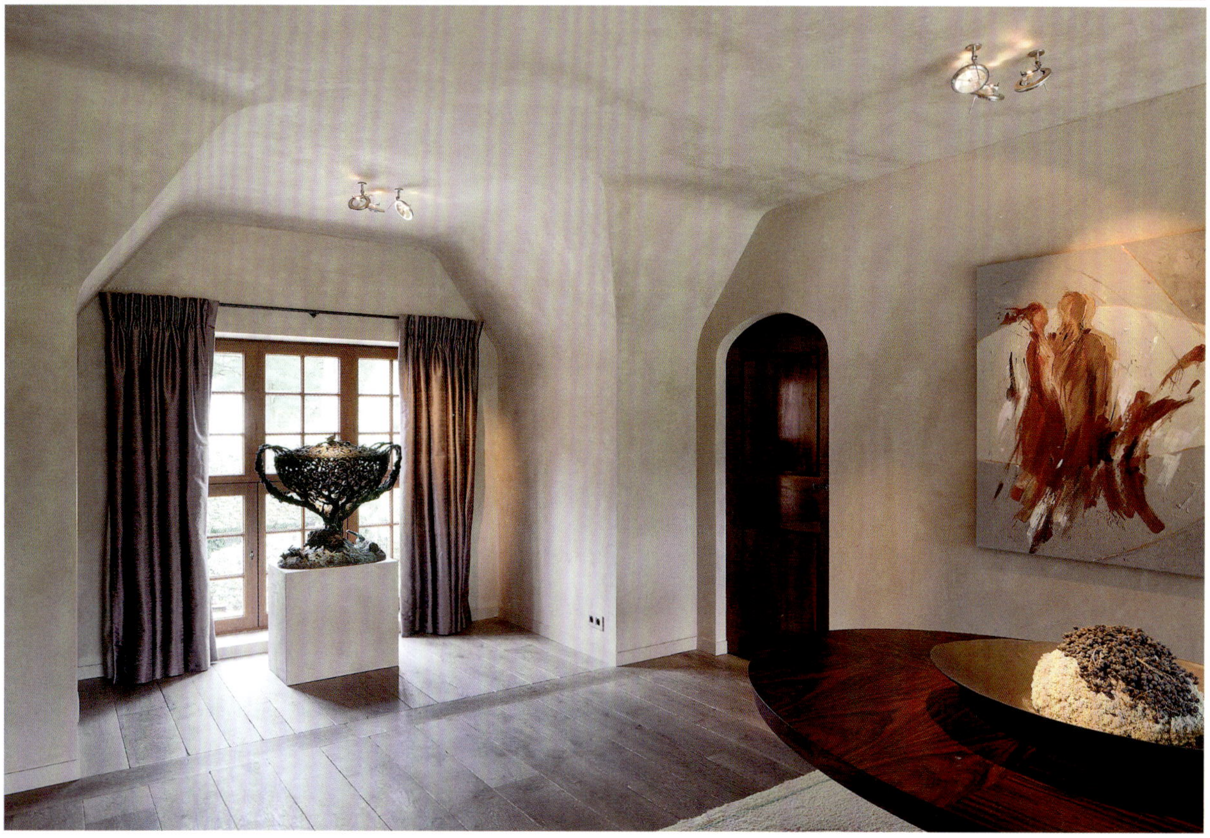

LIGHT, SPACIOUS AND SUNNY

In this house Alexander Cambron, in consultation with architect Luc Toelen, has created a true family home where light, space and a feeling of sunlight prevail. The almost square house has large windows on all sides with views of the garden. The interior decoration was done by Fabienne Dupont. She opted for a sober basis of almost white and nearly black so that colour accents could be added later by the furniture and works of art.

www.alexandershouses.com   www.fabathome.be

The dining table and chairs are from Max Yamamoto.

The kitchen floor is covered with dark brown Woodstone marble. The oak-veneered cabinets were given a dark brown colour. Countertop in sandblasted stone, tap from KWC. The orange bar stools are from Max Yamamoto.

↖
The furniture is from Max Yamamoto (Avenue Louise, Brussels). The artworks were chosen by Yves Ullens (Traqueur the Lumières).

A SYMBIOSIS OF OLD AND NEW

In a small lane in Paris' Triangle d'Or, close to the Plaza Athénée hotel, architect and interior designer Gérard Faivre found a 180m² apartment, which he has renovated from top to bottom. He was aiming to eliminate the bourgeois atmosphere of this very classic place, but at the same time to integrate the authentic elements into a new, contemporary design.

www.gerardfaivreparis.com

The entrance hall with carpet by Toulemonde Bochard; the plum-coloured walls are a striking contrast with the orange of the two Modénature chairs.

The dining-room table is an original piece from Lando, with a metal frame and chairs designed by Paola Navone.

↖
For the double sitting room, Gérard Faivre selected seating by Poltrona Frau, Andrée Putman and Cassina.

203

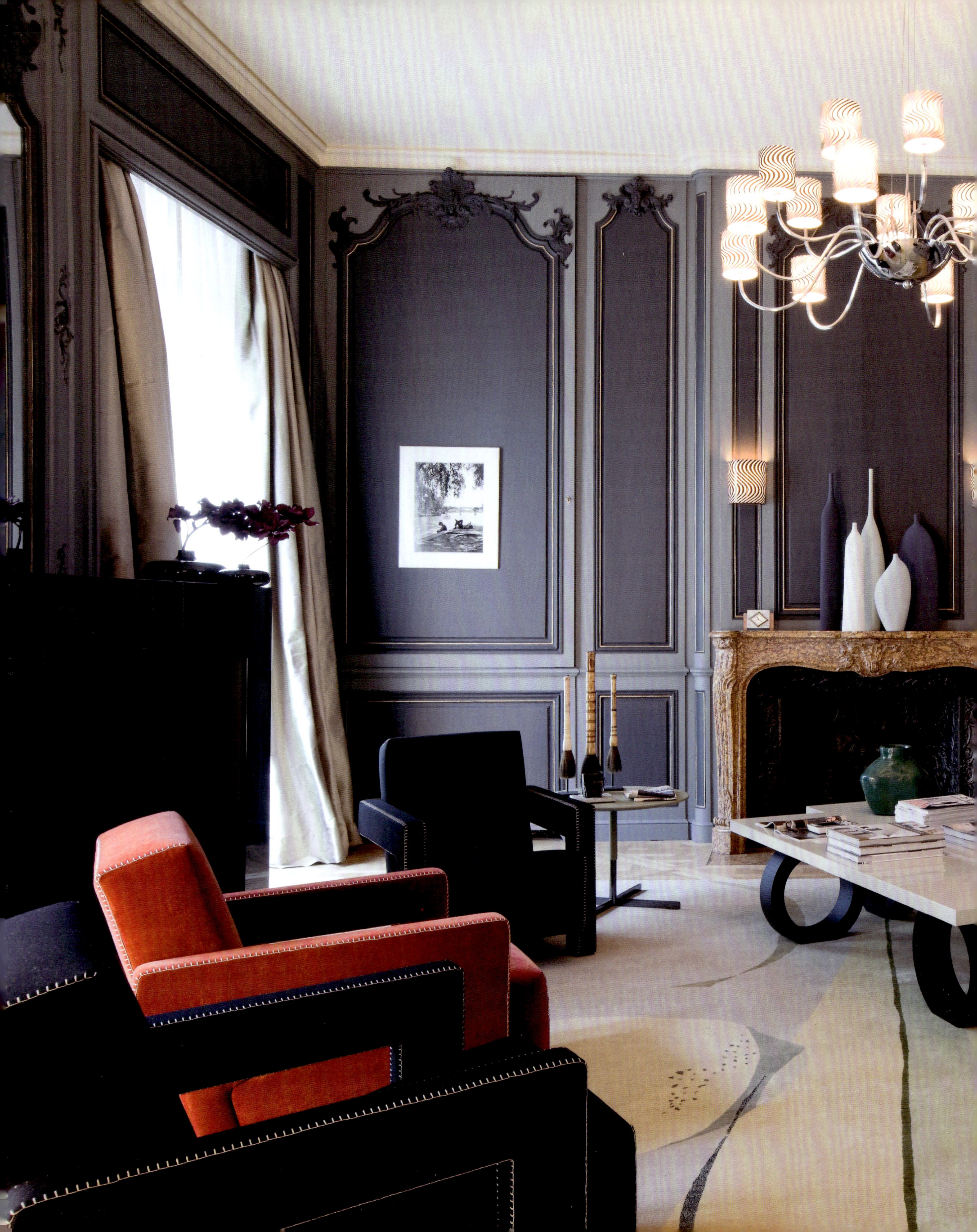

The original marble fireplace has been retained and given a contemporary touch with ceramic vases by Kose.

205

RESTRUCTURING AN APARTMENT IN A HAUSSMANNIAN BUILDING

This apartment, situated in a typical Haussmannian building in Saint-Germain-des-Prés, has been completely restructured by interior architect Anne Derasse with the aim of creating a streamlined, simple look. The apartment has an elongated form, with large glass doors that open onto balconies with beautiful wrought-ironwork and magnificent views. The new windows have completely changed the classic look of the property. The flowing succession of sitting rooms is accentuated by the openings at the side that offer views down the entire length of the apartment, while the openings along the corridor create extra depth.

www.annederasse.be

Above the fireplace, an Indian window from the sixteenth century. Louis XVI chairs in old, patinated leather by Chartier. A large oval Louis XVI table with castors.

The bathroom consists of a pile of blocks containing storage space, with a modern finish in zebrano wood. Dornbracht taps.

↖
A Christian Liaigre sofa in raw linen. The old oak parquet floor in Hungarian point has been polished and given an aged finish.

HAUTE COUTURE IN A HOME IN THE HEART OF PARIS

A few months after the opening of Ebony Interiors' new Paris showroom, Gilles de Meulemeester completed the company's first project in Paris. The result is shown in this report: a sitting room, dining room, TV room, bathroom and bedroom in a home in the heart of Paris where all of the pieces are custom made: Ebony has made such "haute couture" work a company hallmark.

www.ebony-interiors.be

A Broadway dining table and Bruxelles chairs. The radiator grilles, carpet and hanging lamp are custom-made pieces by Ebony.

The walls are painted in stripes.

↖
A carpet in wool, linen and cotton in the TV room.

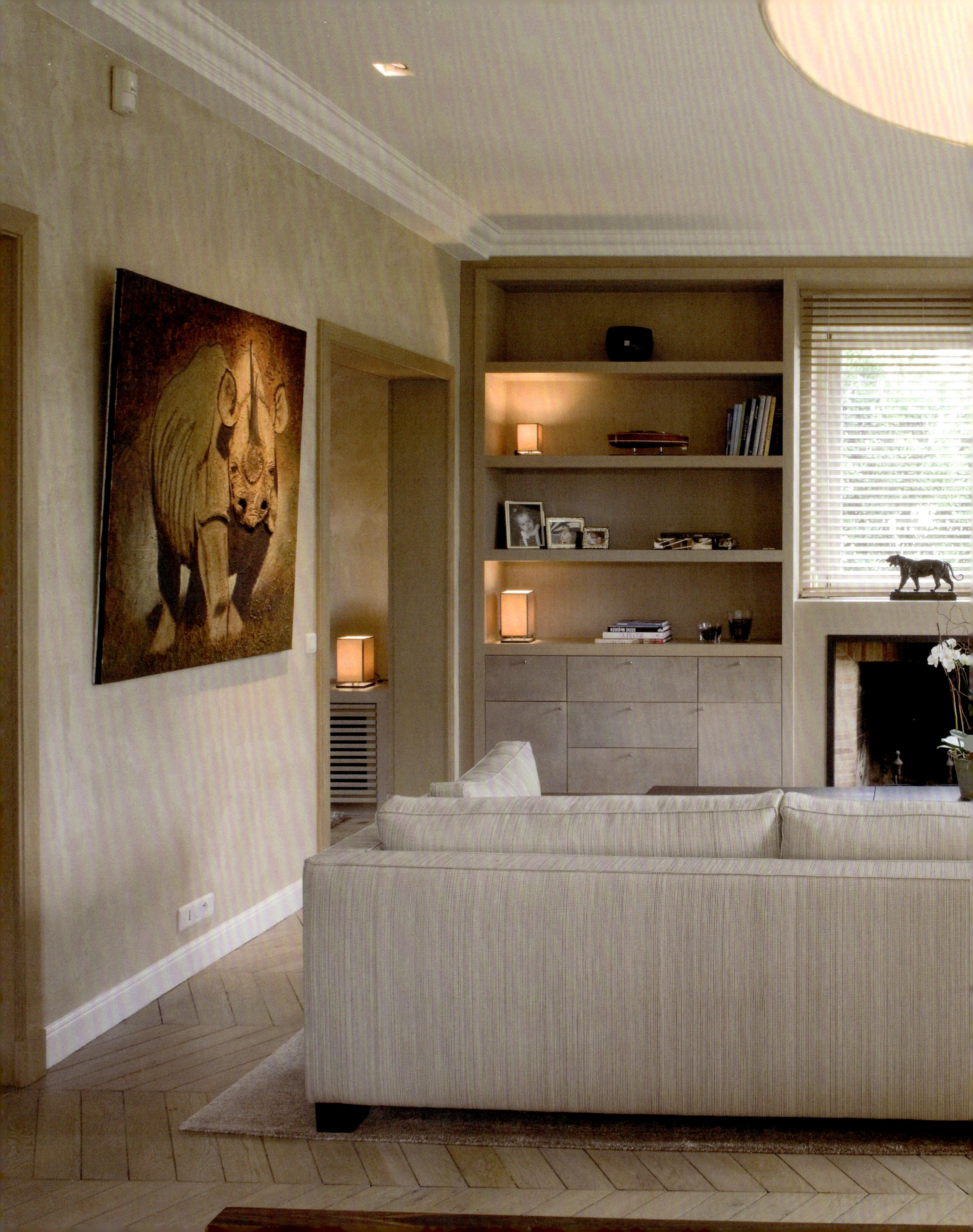

The two Manhattan sofas and the Domino coffee table were made specially by Ebony. The cupboards in the shelving unit are finished in buffalo leather.
The existing Hungarian point floor has been painstakingly restored with a new finish. The walls are in taupe lime paints.
Art (rhinoceros and elephant) by Jean-Philippe Serrano.

SOFT COLOURS IN A RESTORED FARMHOUSE

When the first plans for a new high-speed rail line got known in Hoogmade, it became clear that the old cheese farm dating from 1600 would have to disappear. The existing façade was sawn into pieces and rebuilt at the Open Air Museum in Arnhem. The replica of this farm was rebuilt in Hoogmade, where StyleXclusief established its company. StyleXclusief gives advice on interior styling and techniques making life more comfortable. By using old building materials, soft lime paints, oak wood, concrete and exclusive materials, this cosy farm received a sober and stylish appearance.

www.stylexclusief.nl

Old Chinese lavender chests.

↖
The clinker stone floor, just one centimetre thick, is what makes the entrance hall unique.

The table is made from an old Indian door. The living room is now situated where the cow stables used to be. This explains the number of beams and windows. StyleXclusief substituted the small windows looking onto the garden by high steel doors with large glass windows, providing a vast view over the garden and polders.

Thanks to the natural materials of oak and concrete, the kitchen oozes rural austerity. The beam construction has an aged look by using lime paint.

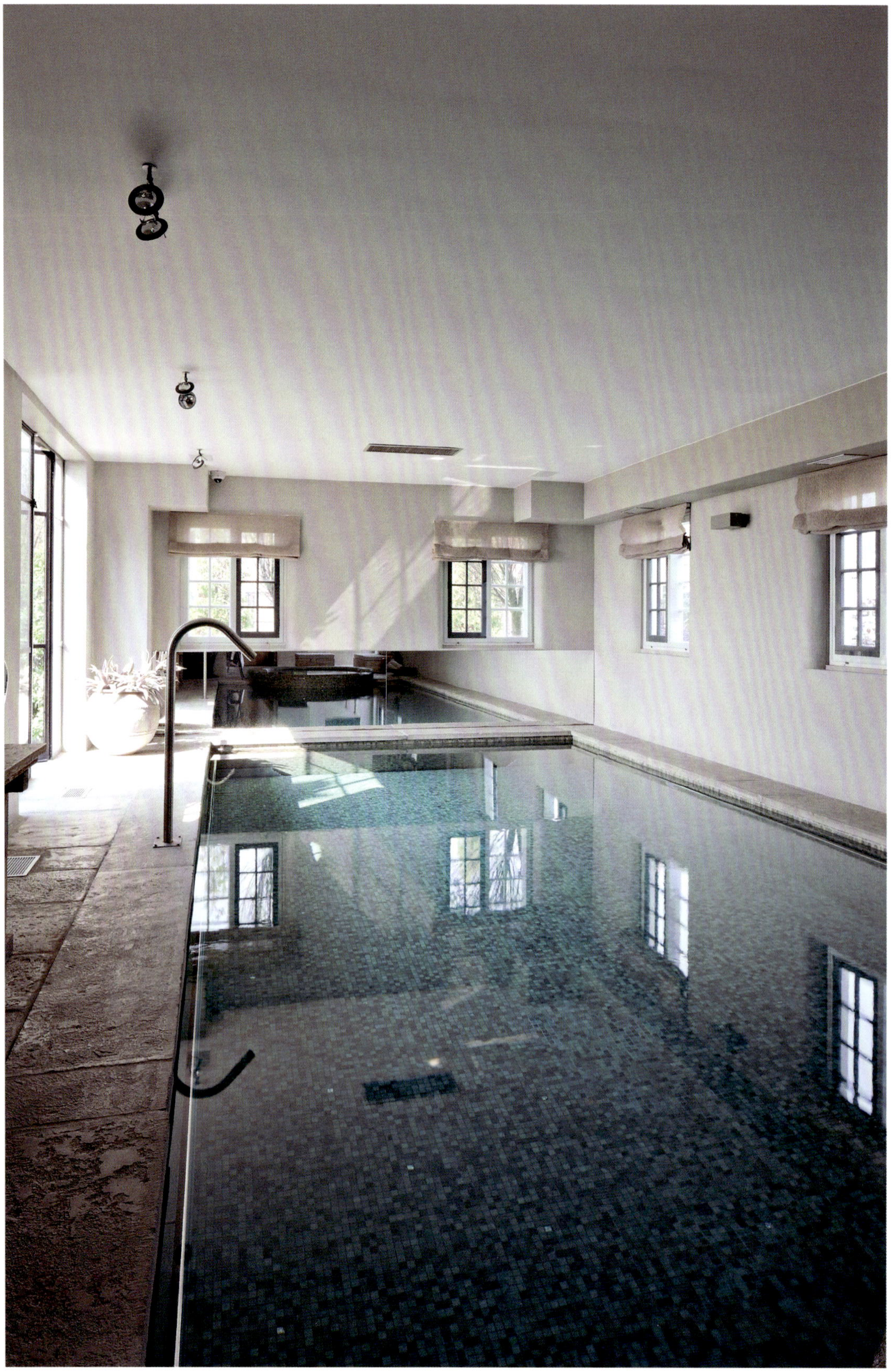

The swimming pool and Turkish bath are tiled with marble mosaic. The fireplace can be operated with an iPad and iPhone.

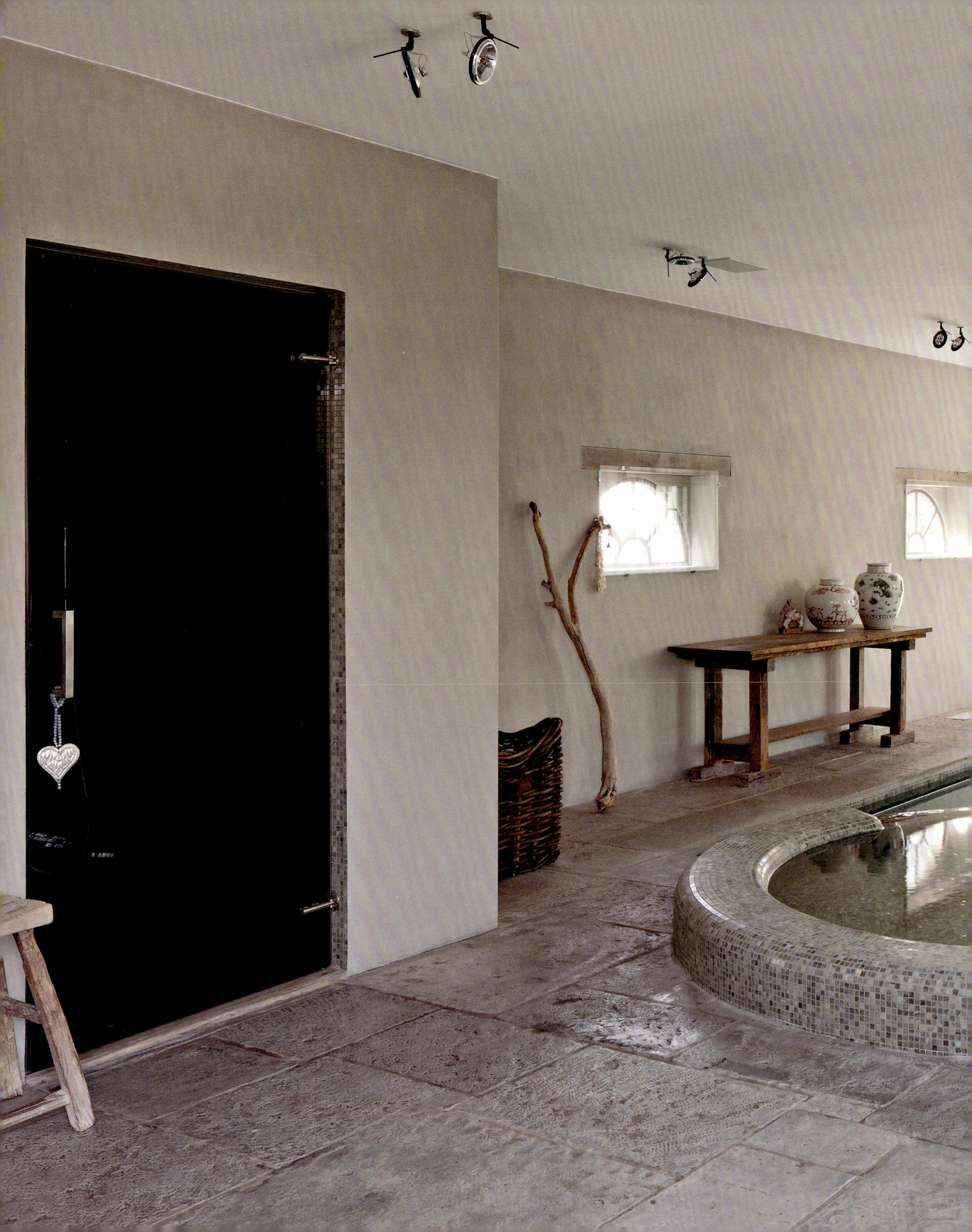

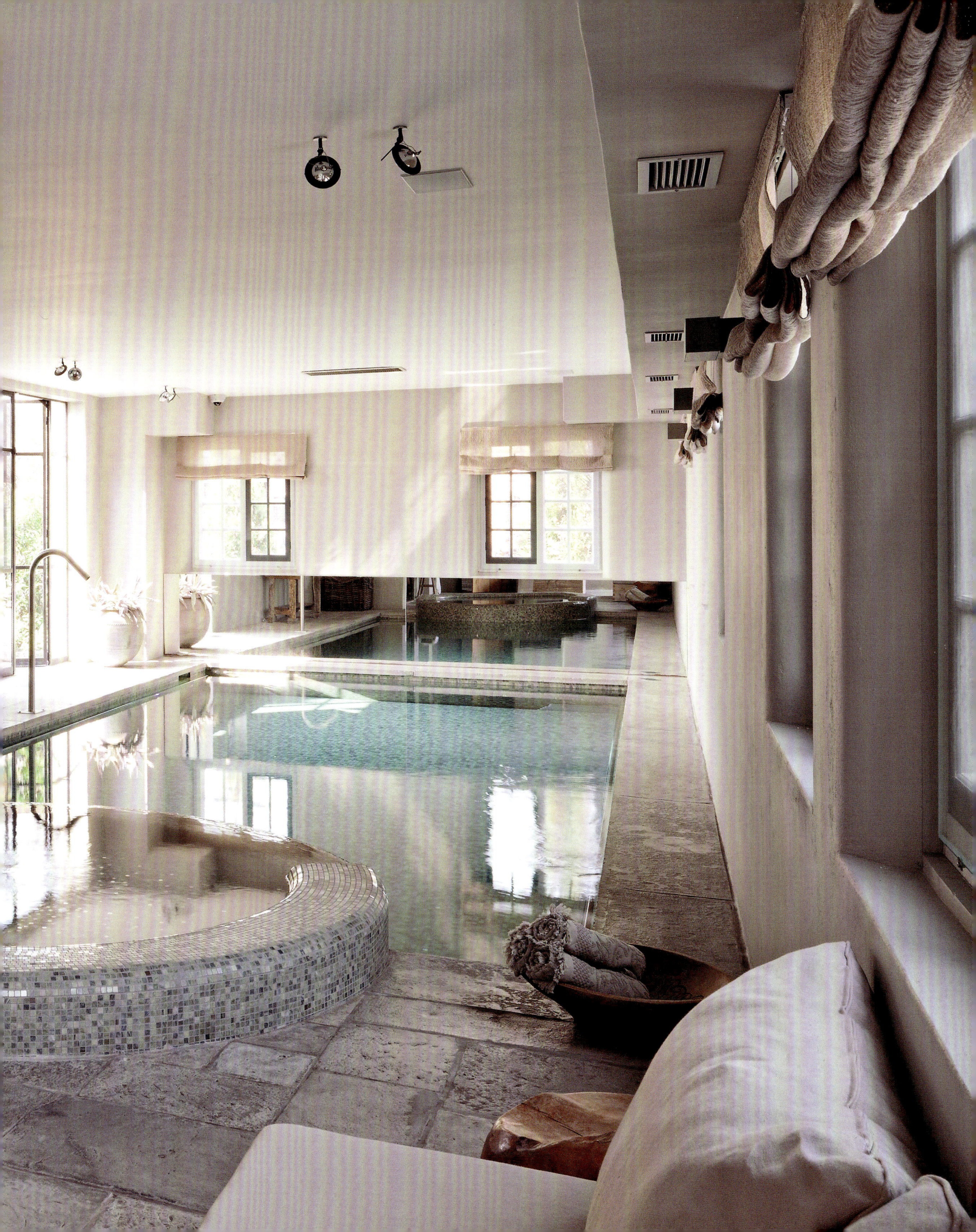

With the smart home electronics, clicking one button is enough to put the whole house to sleep. All lights go out, the thermal blanket of the pool closes and the doors are shut. The guestrooms are decorated with exclusive materials.

The washbasin carved in stone comes from Bali.

An old Indian bridal box.

The washbasin is made of concrete and the walls are coated in tadelakt.

SOURCE OF INSPIRATION

A visit to the updated showroom of Joris Van Apers bvba was a real source of inspiration for the project manager of this project in Damme. He purchased an old, dilapidated and decrepit café in the "Eienbroekstraat" and asked Joris Van Apers to renovate the building into a distinctive and pleasant environment: completely in line with Joris Van Apers' philosophy. After the far-reaching renovation it is a café once again.

www.vanapers.be

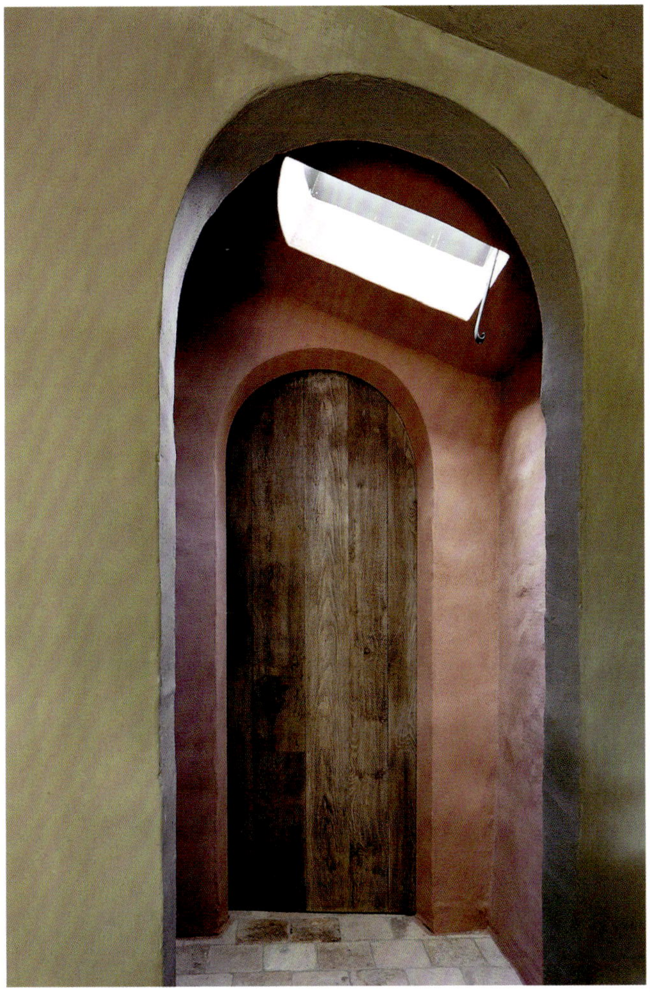

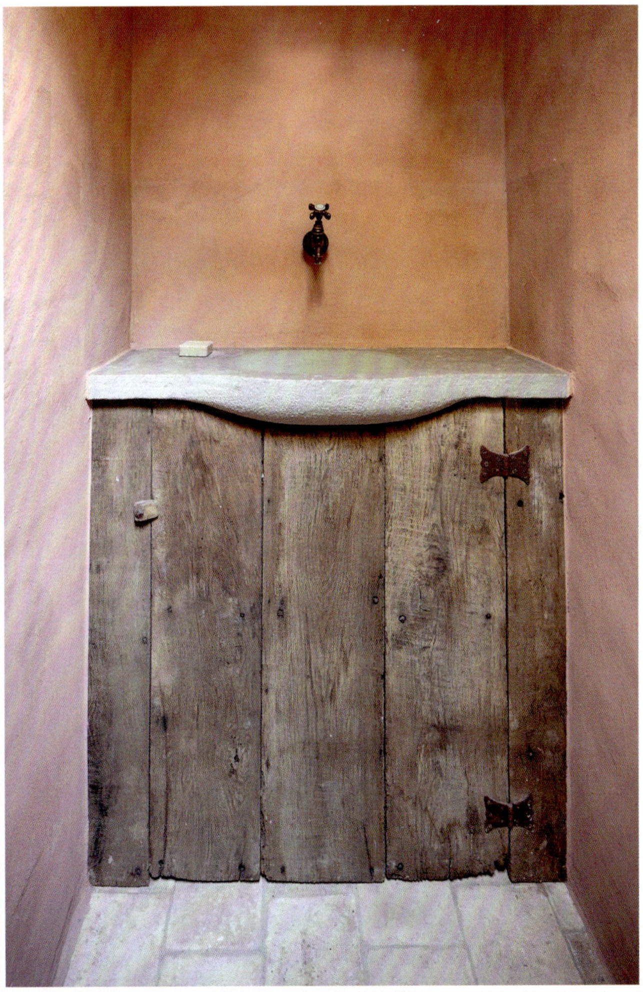

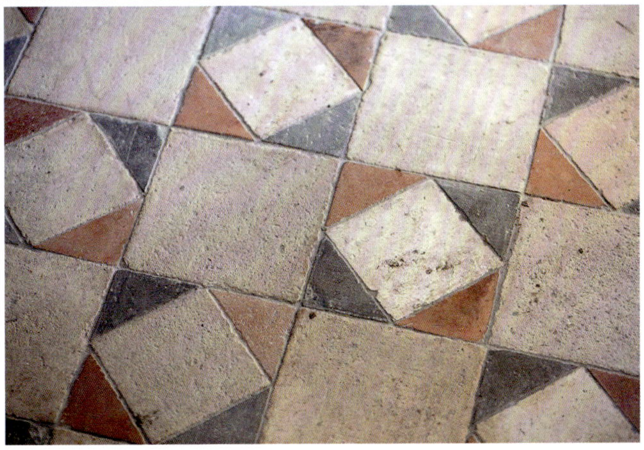

In the centre of the café is a large Louis XIII mantel with Igno-For system (for heat recuperation). A perfect combination with patina walls and recuperated terracotta flooring in light hues. Original Swedish chairs.

The bar. The oak trusses were restored and, where necessary, replaced with old oak beams that are perfectly integrated. Steel interior and exterior windows for lovely glass partition.
Design and realisation by Joris Van Apers bvba.

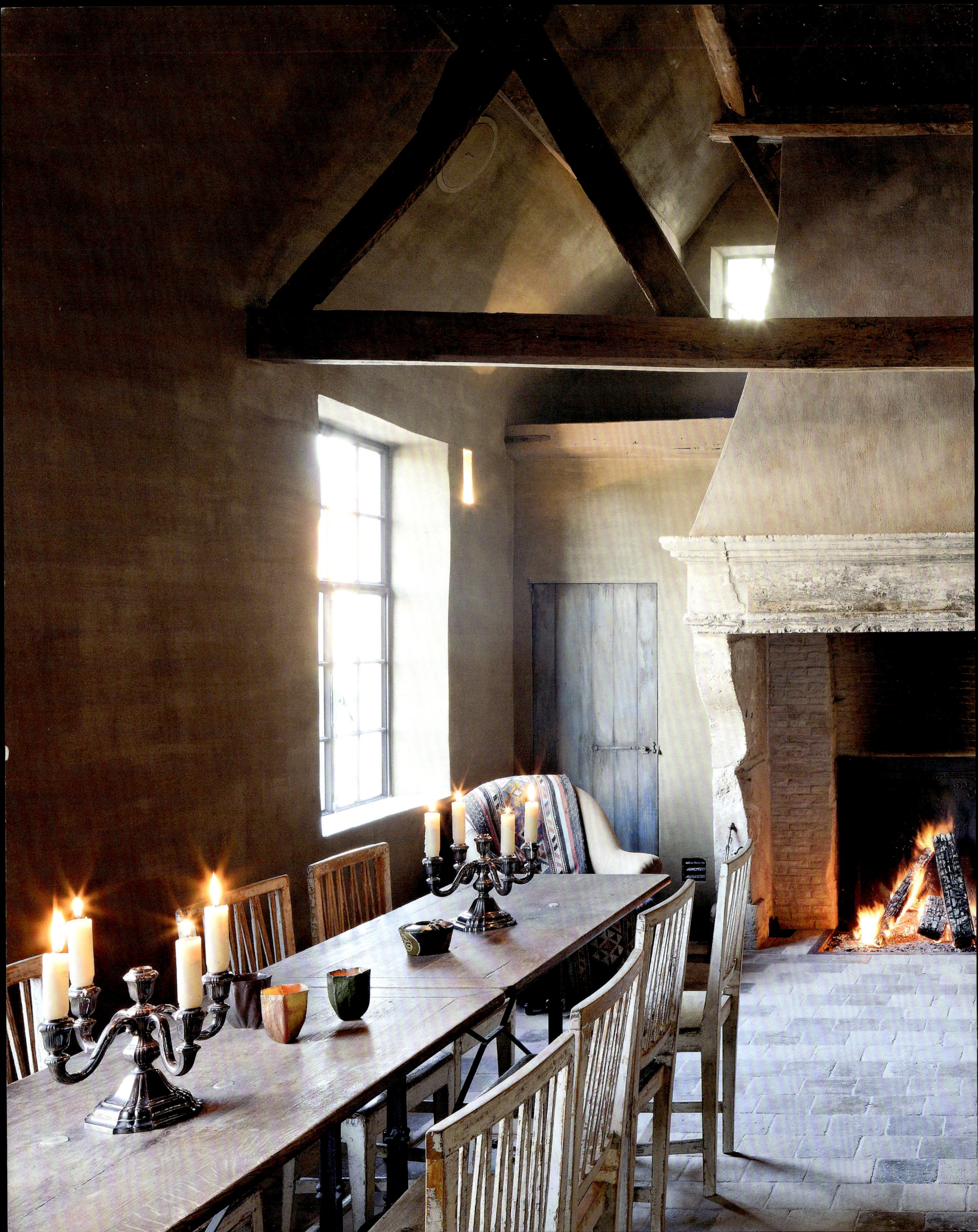

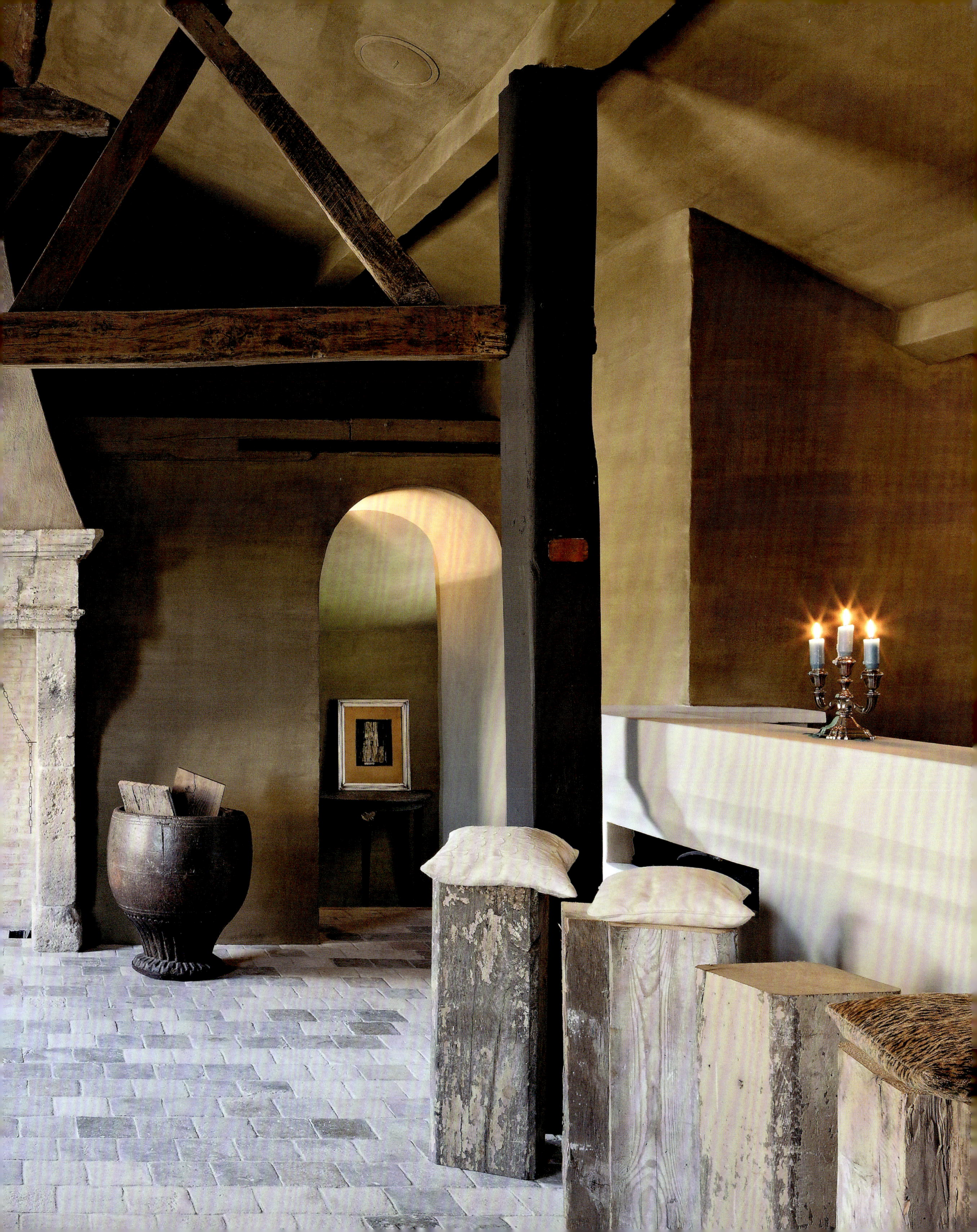

In the lounge, a fireplace with original wood frame and an antique Italian chair. A simple hand-forged handrail and old oak step. The intimate, warm atmosphere is created by the bookshelf made from aged pine, the beautiful beam ceiling and the right aging and paint techniques. Realisation: Joris Van Apers.

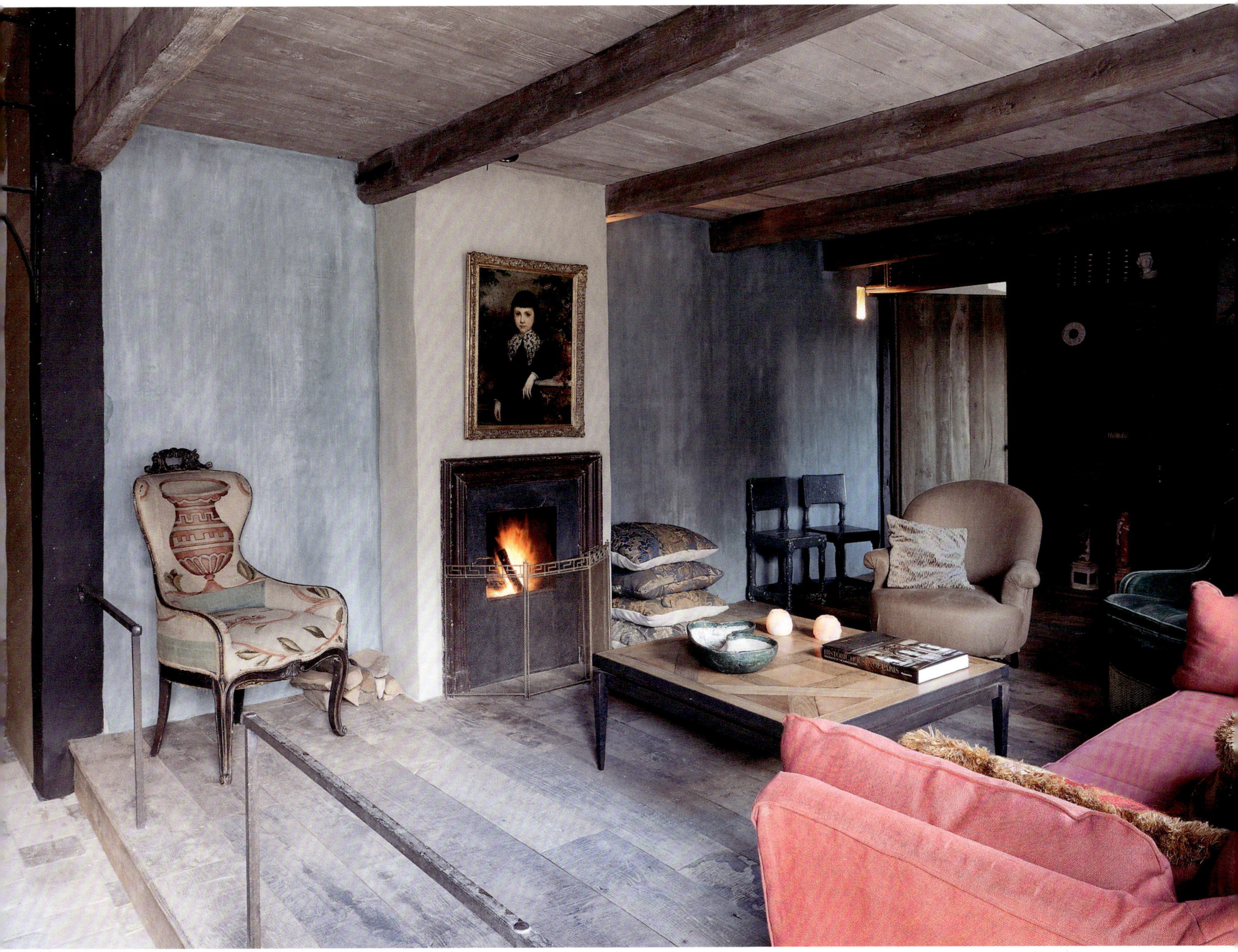

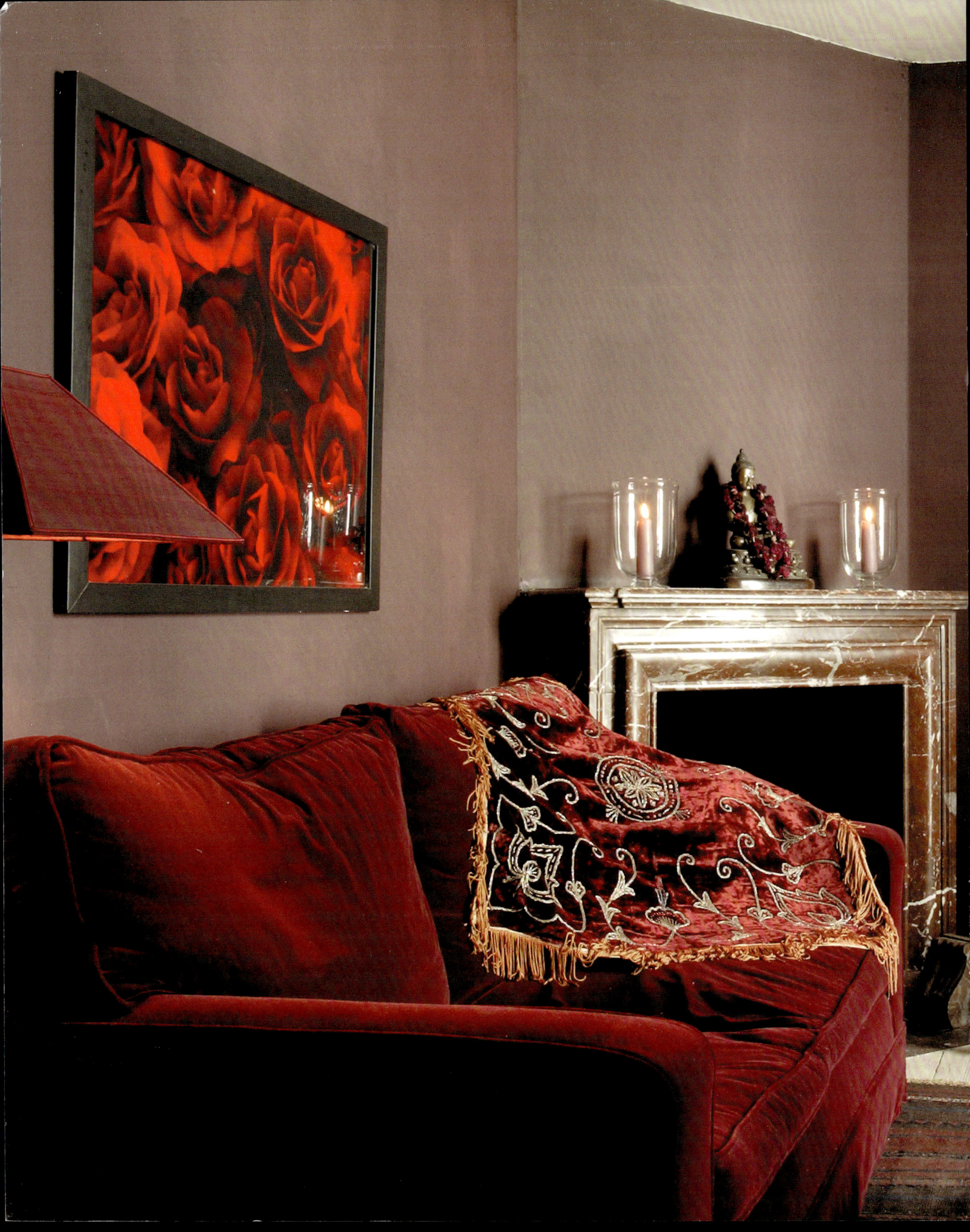

A project by Catherine De Vil. The artwork is by Marie-Jo Lafontaine, «Fleurs de Mal».

PUBLISHER
BETA-PLUS publishing
www.betaplus.com

PHOTOGRAPHY
Jo Pauwels

DESIGN
Polydem – Nathalie Binart

ISBN : 978-90-8944-121-8

© 2013, BETA-PLUS
All rights reserved. No part of this publication may be
reproduced, stored in a retrieval system, or transmitted in any
form or by any means without approval by the publisher.